The Novel As Transformation Myth

The Novel As Transformation Myth

A Study of the Novels of
Mongo Beti and Ngugi wa Thiong'o

Kandioura Dramé

FOREIGN AND COMPARATIVE STUDIES / AFRICAN SERIES 43
MAXWELL SCHOOL OF CITIZENSHIP AND PUBLIC AFFAIRS
SYRACUSE UNIVERSITY

© 1990

MAXWELL SCHOOL OF CITIZENSHIP AND PUBLIC AFFAIRS
SYRACUSE UNIVERSITY, SYRACUSE, NEW YORK 13244-1230

Printed in the United States of America.

We thank the authors, Mongo Beti and Ngugi wa Thiong'o, and their publishers for allowing us to reprint the selections contained in this volume.

Selections from *Remember Ruben* and *Perpetua and the Habit of Unhappiness*, by permission from Mongo Beti; *Lament for an African Pol* (Washington, D. C.: Three Continents Press, 1985), reprinted with the kind permission of the publisher.

Selections from *A Grain of Wheat* and *Weep Not, Child*, by permission from Ngugi wa Thiong'o; *Petals of Blood*, by Ngugi wa Thiong'o, © 1977 by Ngugi wa Thiong'o, reprinted by permission of the publisher, E. P. Dutton, a division of Penguin Books U. S. A, Inc.; *The River Between* (London: Heinemann, 1974) and *Detained: A Writer's Prison Diary* (London: Heinemann, 1981) are reproduced with the kind permission of Heinemann Educational Books, Ltd.

Library of Congress Cataloging-in-Publication Data

Dramé, Kandioura.
    The novel as transformation myth : a study of the novels of Mongo Beti and Ngugi wa Thiong'o / by Kandioura Dramé.
        p.   cm. — (Foreign and comparative studies. African series ; 43)
    Includes bibliographical references.
    ISBN 0-915984-68-7
    1.Beti, Mongo, 1932-   —Criticism and interpretation. 2. Ngugi wa Thiong'o, 1938-   —Criticism and interpretation. 3. African fiction—History and criticism. 4. Metamorphosis in literature. 5. Myth in literature. I. Title. II. Series.
PQ3989.2.B45Z64   1990   7/572   89-14005
843–dc20   CIP

Nfa
Alaji Massirimba Drame
Horomoto

Table of Contents

Preface

Although the two novelists of this study are considered by many to be among the most important novelists of Africa, there have been very few comprehensive studies of their recent novels, either singly or as a group. Many critics have tended to analyze the novels individually.

This study argues that since one of the primary functions of criticism is to help present a complete picture of the writer's vision, the isolationist approach offers, at best, a fragmented image of the writer's worldview. In the cases of Mongo Beti and Ngugi wa Thiong'o, the criticism fails to help the general reader to appreciate their myth-making undertaking as committed writers.

A close study reveals that central to any meaningful assessment of their works is a recognition of three related aspects of their recent creative writing. The first is their use of popular myths and prophecies to lay a foundation for an ambitious narrative project. The second aspect is the writers' presentation of a fictionalized "history" of the Camerounian and Kenyan peoples as a collective quest for freedom. As such, the narratives emphasize the nature of social and class conflicts in their societies in order to capture a historical process in which they are able to associate with other Third World societies. The third aspect is the emergence in the novels of a major narrative innovation in the stylization of oral literature, as the writers seek to create the illusion of an oral narrative by presenting the stories to an imaginary listening audience instead of to readers. In this regard, they also use stylistic elements of the archetypal structure of the traditional initiation process.

When this study was first undertaken, Mongo Beti's *Les deux mères de Guillaume Ismael Dzewatama, futur camionneur* was only being serialized in *Peuples Noirs/Peuples Africains* and Ngugi's *Devil on the Cross* had not been published. These two authors have since published new novels and essays, and I have read and recorded these new books in my bibliography. However, they do not invalidate the present study in any way. If anything, they have at times unexpectedly come to my help by providing more evidence where intuition was once dominant in the ideas I put forth. Thus, the publication of *Devil on the Cross* reinforces the argument that Ngugi's narrative style owes much to oral literature. In the same vein, Beti's *Dictionnaire de la negritude* strengthens my statement about his pan-African empathy. Of the works of criticism recently published on these authors, none addresses their novels as a continuum in the way I do here. So, I felt no need to change the perspective of this study.

The organization of this essay follows a simple plan. It first examines the intellectual and social milieu that informs the creative work of the two writers, it then turns to a study of the role and function of myths in their novels. The following two chapters are devoted to studying the historical vision that emerges from the works as a totality, and the next examines the stylistic innovations that exist in the narratives. The conclusion summarizes the findings of the study and restates the case for the mythopoeic trend to be seen as a powerful stylized statement of a new cultural awareness.

Acknowledgments

I would like to express my deepest gratitude to all the people who took an active interest in this study from its inception and have provided intellectual as well as moral support. Professors Hassan el Nouty and John F. Povey of the University of California at Los Angeles read the dissertation that gave birth to this study and provided valuable comments and guidance. I owe a special gratitude to my friend Professor Aliko Songolo of the University of California at Irvine for his comments on earlier and subsequent versions of this manuscript, and his continuing encouragement and support. My friends Merle L. Bowan and Kenny Marrota graciously took time to read various versions of this book and provided guidance and encouragment for which I am very thankful.

The members of my extended family have done for me more than it is possible to say in these lines. I can only mention their names and hope that they will see this symbolic act as yet another inadequate attempt on my part to thank them from the bottom of my heart: "Big Rob" Whittemore, Elizabeth "Tige" Beverly-Whittemore, Joye "Joie" Bowman, John Higginson, Julie Saville, Abdoulaye "Docteur" Diop, Delyna Hayward Diop, Pape Yoro Tapa Diop, Margaret Brumfield Diop, Lamine "Grand" Keita, Terry Eicher, Ginny Eicher, Judy Francis, Pape and Irene Gaye, Jacques Habib Sy and Yacine Fall, and Ismaila "Izo" Biaye. I also wish to acknowlededge all my friends at *Ufahamu* who provided a permanent "Africa forum" around the journal.

I would especially like to thank Phillip Burham for providing the initial means to undertake the studies that led to the writing of this book and, at the University of Virginia, the Carter G. Woodson Institute for Afro-American and African Studies for providing material and moral support in the writing of this book, in particular Dr. Armstead L. Robinson, Dr. William E. Jackson, Mary F. Rose, and Gail Shirley.

Last, but not least, I wish to thank my editors, Professors K. C. Morisson and Peter Castro, and especially Joanna Giansanti, for their patient and expert guidance throughout the preparation of this book.

1

Introduction

The history of African literatures is yet to be written. More and more, the multifaceted character of the literatures is revealed by writers, and the days are over when one person could claim to know African literature in its breadth and scope; from orature and its diverse genres to written literatures both ancient and modern, not to speak of its multifarious connections with other world literatures, music and dance, painting and sculpture, it represents a vast and fertile land. Yet, to the attentive student of Africa's cultural life, it still seems to be "morning yet on creation day," simply because so many works of breath-taking beauty continue to appear.

Is it, paradoxically, the very exuberance of the creative works that often stuns their readers into stupor and sometimes inertia? For the criticism of African literatures has not always lived up to the challenge of the artists. In the seductive and comfortable shade of the radiant Negritude palaver tree, many critics boldly hammered home with the startling innocence of certainty the idea that lyrical poetry naturally precedes prose narrative. Notwithstanding the erroneous nature of the claim in the specific case of contemporary African literature, the unanimity of voices that resulted from this activity succeeded, for a while, in relegating the African novel—especially the novel written in French—into oblivion. Its sudden death was loudly deplored much in the same way that theater today is said to be dead. Meanwhile, however, the novel continued to flourish; but if a particular work could not be fitted into the dubious parameters of traditional versus modern life, alienation versus authenticity, or the colonial/anticolonial scheme, it was often ignored. Useful as these parameters may be when handled judiciously, the critics have not always succeeded in extending them to take stock of the aesthetic principles at work in the novels.

In many cases, questions of artistic innovations were treated incidentally, if not altogether neglected. But with writers like Mongo Beti and Ngugi wa Thiong'o who continue to reinvent the novel, the barrenness of this kind of "ready-made" criticism becomes all too obvious and in some instances even forbidding. These writers are trendsetters, and their creative work cannot be kept within the confines of simple schemes.

To be sure, bringing Beti and Ngugi together is, for me, less than a fanciful or fortuitous act. It is informed by the arresting fact that these two writers have created what I must call "the novel as transformation myth," the metaphoric expression of accomplished, as well as projected, collective and individual mutations; and they have done so beautifully and convincingly. This creative undertaking at once sets them apart from, and unites them with, other novelists, as a careful reader is bound to recognize all the themes and many of the techniques already present in African novels in the novels that form the material of this study. The syncretic alchemy here remains, however, their distinguishing mark and the force of their outstanding achievement.

In addition to helping the reader appreciate more the originality of the novels of Beti and Ngugi, it is also hoped that this comparative study will shed light on the growing trend of the cyclical novel among African writers. Mohamed Dib, Chinua Achebe, and the late Tchicaya U Tam'Si, among others have experimented with the cyclical novel, but never before has it attained such a high level of assurance, consistency, and homogeneity as it does in the novels that form the nexus of the present study. The urge of these writers to compose a cyclical novel is born of a desire to boldly capture in a vivid depiction Africa's successful and desired transformations. The novels, then, offer their ideal audience a picture of its cultural identity in its mutative form in a manner that is both unsettling and exhilarating.

In order to achieve this goal, Beti and Ngugi had to exercise a profound skepticism in the face of the current political discourse of African officials and their advisers (many of whom are European), a discourse that is aimed at painting a harmonious, static image of Africa while the societies are torn by tremendous upheavals. They observe Africa's cultural life with a critical eye as befits responsible, committed artists. And it is from this posture that they proceed to debunk many dangerous myths even as they construct transformational ones. They are visionary novelists whose enterprise of demystification does not leave a void. On the contrary, it is filled with a positive mythology created from the ashes of the old ones and the seeds of new or renewed aspirations.

Visionary Sensibility and Myth-Making

Mongo Beti and Ngugi wa Thiong'o are two of Africa's most outstanding novelists. Although they have both received a fair degree of critical attention, most of the criticism has failed to study their novels as a continuum. This is a crucial aspect of the works since it shows the unity of the specific vision that informs Beti's return to fiction after a decade of literary silence and the driving force behind most of Ngugi's writing. Few critics of Beti or Ngugi have seen their novels as trilogies, and those who mention it do not go beyond the simple statement of the fact.[1]

Yet, in the course of this study, it became obvious to me that the novels find their unity in the almost repetitive evocation of a central symbol. For Beti, this is the symbolic universe that the name "Ruben" summons forth; the central symbol is therefore linked with the heroic struggle of the Camerounian people for freedom. For Ngugi, the central symbol is the Mau Mau quest for land and freedom. Since these symbols link three novels closely together in each case, I have found it appropriate to interpret each set of novels as a trilogy, i.e., three novels that can be read as one unified narrative. In the case of Beti, I call the narrative the Ruben trilogy, and in the case of Ngugi, the Mau Mau trilogy.[2]

To date, there have been very few comprehensive studies of their recent novels, either singly or as a group. Many critics have tended to analyze the novels individually. It is the argument of this study that since one of the primary functions of criticism is to help present a complete picture of the vision of the writer, the isolationist approach offers, at best, a fragmented image of the writer's worldview. In the cases of Mongo Beti and Ngugi wa Thiong'o, the criticism has failed to help the general reader to appreciate their myth-making undertaking as committed writers.

A close study reveals that central to any meaningful assessment of their works is a recognition of three related aspects of their recent creative writing. The first one is their use of popular myths and prophecies to lay a foundation for an ambitious narrative project. The second aspect is the writers' presentation of a fictionalized "history" of the Camerounian and Kenyan peoples as a collective quest for freedom. As such, the narratives emphasize the nature of social and class conflicts in their societies in order to capture a historical process with which they are able to associate other Third World societies. The third aspect is the emergence in the novels of a major narrative innovation in the stylization of orature, as the writers seek to create the illusion of an oral narrative by presenting the stories to an imaginary audience instead of readers. In this regard, they also use stylistic elements of the archetypal structure of the traditional initiation process.

Beti's interest in depicting processes of social transformation in Africa can be traced back to his first published story. He was only twenty-one years old, and this story is still one of the rare stories on the Mau Mau revolution written in French by an African. "Sans haine et sans amour," published in *Présence Africaine* under the pseudonym of Eza Boto, is a short story about a young Mau Mau freedom fighter ordered to finish off a wounded chief, a collaborator of the colonial government.[3] Although this piece is undeniably a beginner's first step, it does contain elements that foreshadow the recent "Ruben novels." The Mau Mau movement became the main focus of Ngugi, while Beti has not returned to this subject. However, both writers share a great interest in the exploration of the African past. Ngugi, for example, views this exploration as a mission of the writer.

> We, as writers, as historians, as Kenyan intellectuals must be able to tell stories, or histories, or a history of heroic resistance to foreign domination by Kenyan people.[4]

It is this notion of fiction as stories, as a heroic history, that forms the nexus of the present study. As stories that combine historical realism and the deliberate, though not arbitrary, choice of the writers to depict a heroic story, the novels rely on myths and prophecies to lay a foundation for the narratives that are considered here. The link between myth and history in the dramatization of the past in these narratives is mediated by a realistic portrayal of actual and possible social transformations.

In defining myth, I have focused on its functional role as a narrative of creation, discovery, and transformation by emphasizing its dynamic nature. The definition adopted by Gilbert Durand has been most helpful in circumscribing myth as a dynamic narrative of historical and legendary tenor. In doing so, he correctly rejects the more restrictive definition of myth as a system of ritual representations only. Taken in its broader sense, as Durand does, myth designates "a dynamic system of symbols, of archetypes and schemes the very mechanism of which disposes it to narrative composition." He also indicates that the expressiveness of myth is often mediated through words and ideas. Thus, he states, "Myth is already a form of rationalization because it uses the mode of discourse which converts symbols into words and archetypes into ideas." As such, it paves the way for legend and the historical narrative.[5]

Césaire, who has had an earlier and quite successful acquaintance with the mythopoeic vision based on historical figures that are transformed into heroic and legendary characters, adopts a similar view in placing myth in the context of the work of imagination. Like Durand, Césaire—the author of *La Tragédie du roi Christophe* and *Une saison au Congo*—stresses the dynamism of myths as narratives that are affective and rational, and are thus endowed with a particular force that necessarily involves movement, therefore transformations.[6] In the context of the narratives I endeavor to study here, it is important to underline the transformational dynamism that animates the works in order to interpret them in their full scope.

In his seminal essay, "The West Indian Writer and His Quarrel with History," Edward Baugh shows how history is an ever-present preoccupation of the writers in their exploration of contemporary Caribbean life.[7] This interest, though not exclusive to Caribbean and African writers, has a peculiar resonance here, due perhaps to the colonial experience.

The contemporary African writer's concern with the African present sometimes finds its literary expression in the dramatization of the past.[8] Several centuries of colonialism have radically changed the course of African history. The economic exploitation of Africa was conducted simultaneously with an ideological coercion designed to distort African history. Africa is, therefore, confronted with the formidable task of re-forming this history. For this reason, the African writer is often faced with the necessity to reconsider, evaluate, and interpret African history. In this exegesis, the writer may emphasize the positive aspects of the history. He delves into the past to retrieve seemingly dead legends and myths in an attempt to revitalize them. But sometimes he simply seizes a historical moment that he dramatizes as myth.

Beti, for example, makes a great effort to rescue the memory of such great historical figures as Ruben Um Nyobe from the prison house of censorship and complicity of silence, while Ngugi strives to correct the deformed image often presented of Jomo Kenyatta. It is very disturbing that despite his documented contribution to Cameroun and the rest of Africa, Ruben Um Nyobe is still ignored by official Camerounian literature where historical figures of the country's struggle for self-rule are concerned and that he is still belittled in history books endorsed for schools or allowed within the country. And although Kenyatta was widely seen in Africa as a great leader when Ngugi wrote *A Grain of Wheat*, it was still necessary to present him as such in the novel in order to counterbalance the powerful British media that had, largely through colonial literature and the press, depicted Kenyatta and the Land and Freedom Army as an irrational and blood-thirsty bunch.

The act of recreating legends and myths hinges on three variables. The writer may use an ancient or popular myth that he endeavors to adapt to a given situation. He may also choose to use historical characters. In this case, he seeks to elevate the legendary figures to a mythical level. Finally, he may use both types in his narrative complex.

According to Claude Meillassoux, these myths present, in general, three types of events: genesis, discovery, and transformation. A genesis myth often describes the origin of a world and its humanity, whereas a discovery myth may depict the discovery of a technique or the invention of a tool. As a mode of cultural expression, a transformation myth symbolically reflects social changes.[9] In so doing, it assumes a historical backdrop to the story. It depicts social transformations that are brought into being harmoniously or conflictingly. It offers an explanation of the process whereby a social condition is established through a mutation of social relations. In the trilogies under study here, the struggle for power between the social forces controls the narrative impetus and appears as the *sine qua non* for the advent of freedom and justice.

Because of the complexity of the subject under study, I have adopted an approach that is as global as possible, even at the risk of appearing eclectic. I have tried to define the function of the myths and prophecies in the narratives. Secondly, I have endeavored to unveil the internal dynamism that animates the narratives in their epic-like unraveling as the expression of a collective—and individual—quest for freedom. Thirdly, I have examined the syntax of the quest through a study of the narrative styles that permit the successful progression of the fictionalized quest.

There is a correlation between this literary expression and the writers' political commitment, as a few of the crucial milestones along their itineraries will indicate. Without writing a biographical sketch of these two writers—a project beyond the scope of this modest study—it is still important for the comparative perspective to show what sets them apart and what unites them. In the process, it will also become obvious that their intellectual and social backgrounds have sharpened their cultural awareness and literary expression.

Two Writers and Their Milieu

Although profound cultural similarities bind African peoples across the continent, a hasty generalization of literary expressions may be regrettable. The differences between the cultures should always be taken into account. In the context of this study, it is necessary to be aware of three important differences between the two writers and their cultural milieu. These differences are linguistic, historical, and individual.

The linguistic differences are profound. Whereas Beti always writes in French, Ngugi now writes in both English and Gikuyu. The shift to Gikuyu starts with *Ngaahika Ndenda*,[10] a play that prompted the Kenyan government to detain Ngugi. He has subsequently written and published a novel in Gikuyu.[11] However, all the novels that form the focus of the present study have been written in English. Like many African writers, Beti writes in French although he speaks his native Beti. Like Ngugi, he has taken a strong position against linguistic and cultural imperialism, especially with regard to French, as far back as 1974, when he allowed the narrator of *Perpetua* to make the following observation:

> As in colonial times, but today with all the presumption and complacency of 'aid to underdeveloped countries,' the minds of Africa's young people were being withered and desiccated by the superfluous, almost frivolous aridities of a foreign language, itself in any case discredited by centuries of overt or concealed slavery. *Meanwhile, the languages of the Africans themselves, the treasure houses of their genius, their own proper and irreplaceable means of expression, consigned to the perpetual status of vernaculars, had been suppressed, relegated and proscribed.* (p. 91; my emphasis)

Nearly a decade later, Beti published an important essay on African languages and French cultural imperialism.[12] In this essay, he provides a survey of the history of the French language in Africa, from the colonial era to the present. The essay is at once a critique of French imperialism disguised as a low-grade commonwealth of French speakers under the name of Francophonie, a demystification of French expatriates disguising themselves as linguists interested in the promotion of African languages or so-called experts in African affairs, and a debunking of the myth of the unsuitability of African languages for abstract expression.

Beti shows how the dominant position of the French language in Africa goes hand in hand with the political manipulation of African countries by France and its exploitation of their resources. Clearly, the continued domination of the French language over indigenous African languages contributes to the growing "bantustanization" of African peoples and cultures.

The novelist makes a plea in favor of indigenous African languages so that they may, once again, play the noble functions that they played before the colonial era. He expresses a need for an effective decolonization and Africanization by Africans of the French language. In his view, much of the hostility of a people toward a colonial language only disappears when the people regain a position of independence from which they can freely choose to use that language to serve their own purposes. Beti points to the case of India as an example of a country that has successfully revised its relationship to the English language. But considering that the former colonies of France in sub-Saharan Africa have not even come close to realizing such a revision, Beti cautions young Africans from these countries against a hasty decision and expresses the view that the relationship between African languages and French belongs in the area of accommodation rather than divorce.

After qualifying his essay as a modest contribution to the vast subject of the linguistic problems of Africa, Beti concludes with a strong statement in favor of the use of African languages. In particular, he notes that the need to change from colonial languages to indigenous African languages is not merely a matter of technical opportunity, but a matter of collective survival. The peoples of so-called "Francophone Africa" are faced with the necessity of rehabilitating their languages or running the risk of being petrified, condemned to a slow but inexorable death.

Although Beti and Ngugi speak about the same need, the emphasis is different. Whereas Ngugi boldly demands the unilateral and unconditional use of indigenous African languages in all areas of African affairs, particularly in literature, Beti advocates giving priority in Africa to literature written in French by Africans over literature written in French by European writers. Beyond recognizing the necessity of rehabilitating African languages, there is a big difference between these two positions.

In a sense, Beti has admitted that there are flaws in his views on this subject by publishing a critique of his own essay. The critique titled "Y'a bon français africain," written by Karim Traoré and Jean-Claude Naba, takes Beti to task for failing to envision the possibility of African literature in indigenous African languages in his essay on African languages and French cultural imperialism.[13] They point to a number of startling contradictions in Beti's essay, including his idea of a situation of accommodation between French and African languages instead of a divorce.

In the conclusion of their strong critique, the authors demand that progressive African intellectuals revise their attitude toward African languages. They maintain that the problem of African languages demands as much commitment as does the struggle against the political and economic exploitation of Africa; therefore, they warn against the kind of prioritization that assumes that the resolution of political and economic difficulties will automatically solve the language problem.

The question of "language" in the study of African literature is very important. Although it continues to draw diverse reactions from writers and readers, a full discussion of the subject is beyond the scope of this essay. It is important, however, to underline here the fact that one of the direct consequences of the linguistic difference between Beti and Ngugi is the serious limitations it poses on the ability of the writers themselves to communicate outside of the help of translations.[14]

Another difference is the historical difference of colonialism in Kenya and Cameroun. Although Cameroun has suffered the combined effects of German and then British and French colonial rules, Kenya has suffered in a special way from the sole British settler colonialism. In this regard, the Kenyan experience is closer to those of Algeria, Zimbabwe, and South Africa.

Kenya was declared a British protectorate in 1895. A railway running from Mombasa to Kampala was built, cutting through the Kenya Highlands where the Gikuyu, Maasai, and Wakamba peoples lived. According to George Padmore, "the British Governor General Sir Charles Eliot appealed to the Englishmen of the gentry class to come out to Kenya and settle as gentlemen farmers."[15] By 1955, there were 30,000 British settlers and 16,000 square miles of the most productive land were appropriated by 2,000 settlers. Only 52,000 square miles of mostly arid or semiarid land had been set aside for 5.5 million Africans. By introducing taxation and forced labor, the colonial government created farm workers out of a dispossessed African peasantry. In the "White Highlands," many Africans, especially Gikuyus, became "squatters" (resident laborers) on estates,[16] while others worked for Europeans on a seasonal or temporary basis. The colonial government also placed racial restrictions on growing certain cash crops, particularly coffee and tea. Thus, the settlers controlled the total production of cash crops.

This land situation is one of the root causes of the Mau Mau uprising in 1952. While settlers coined rules to appropriate land from African peasants, the indigenous people began organizing against and fighting colonial rule. In 1922, the East African Association was formed; it was led courageously by a Gikuyu named Harry Thuku in protest against the eviction of Africans from the Highlands. The heroic figure of Harry Thuku caught the imagination of Ngugi.

> This Harry Thuku has already moved into patriotic heroic legends and I have treated him as such in the early chapters of my novel, *A Grain of Wheat.*[17]

In 1928, the Kikuyu Central Association was formed, and Jomo Kenyatta became its secretary. It demanded the restitution of the land to African peasants; the colonial government eventually responded to the demand by suppressing the organization in 1939. In 1947, Kenya African Union (K.A.U.) was formed around the same land issue. According to Padmore, by 1952, the landless Africans had formed a large urban lumpen-proletariat.

In October 1952, when Ngugi was fourteen years old, the government declared the State of Emergency in Kenya in order to suppress the Land and Freedom Army, which became known as Mau Mau. The "independent" schools that had been established by Africans were closed. The African Teachers Training College was also closed, and its founder, Mbiyu Koinange,[18] was arrested as a Mau Mau suspect. Kenyatta and at least twenty-five other officers of K.A.U. were arrested on 20 October 1952. This same Kenyatta is glorified as the saviour in Ngugi's earliest Mau Mau novel.[19]

Dedan Kimathi, a landless Gikuyu, led the Mau Mau freedom fighters into the forests and mountains of Kenya for a fierce guerilla warfare that did not end until 1958. Young Ngugi lived through the bloody war, and his brother took part in it, while his mother was detained by the enemy. Ngugi remembers the devastation the war had caused:

> I came back after the first term and confidently walked back to my old village. My home was now only a pile of dry mud-stones, bits of grass, charcoal and ashes. Nothing remained, not even crops, except for a lone pear tree that slightly swayed in sun and wind. I stood there bewildered. Not only my home, but the old village with its culture, its memories and its warmth had been razed to the ground. I walked up the ridge not knowing whither I was headed until I met a solitary old woman. Go to Kamiriithu, she told me. Kamiriithu was. . . the name of a new "emergency village" . . . all around me I saw women and children on rooftops with hammers and nails and poles and thatch, building the new homes because their men were in detention camps or away with the people's guerilla army. Many critics have noted the dominance of the theme of return in my novels, plays and short stories, particularly in *A Grain of Wheat*.[20]

In his Mau Mau trilogy, Ngugi chronicles the struggle that opposed the settlers and the Kenyan peasants. If the theme of the restitution of the land is so central to his writing, it is because the land issue is the focal point and the root cause of the war against settler colonialism in Kenya.

As for Cameroun, it had been a German colony before World War I. At the end of the war, the French and the English occupied Cameroun, which, like Togoland, became a League of Nations mandate and United Nations trust territory after World War II. The country was divided into two parts, the majority of which was placed under French trusteeship and the remainder under British administration.

The Union des Populations du Cameroun (U.P.C.) was formed in 1948. According to Richard A. Joseph, it

> was the only major political party to emerge in French sub-Saharan Africa which demanded from the first years of its existence independence from France and the French Union as its main and unalterable goal.[21]

The U.P.C. drew its support mainly from three social formations, particularly in the southern part of the country (the native region of Mongo Beti). It was supported by the Union des Syndicats Confédérés du Cameroun (U.S.C.C.), the country's trade union organization, led by Ruben Um Nyobe until he took up the position of secretary general of the U.P.C. Even the most casual reading of Beti's own essay on the decolonization of Cameroun in *Main basse sur le Cameroun*[22] will recognize his admiration for the principal leader of the Camerounian struggle for freedom. But it is instructive to also consider the opinion of a scholar who is neither French nor Camerounian, but rather a Caribbean scholar of socio-political life in Cameroun during the U.P.C. years.

> He (Ruben Um Nyobe) was undoubtedly one of the most brilliant political thinkers and organizers to emerge after the Second World War in Africa. Had he survived to lead his country to independence, he would have most certainly been ranked today on the same level as Julius Nyerere, and the late Kwameh Nkrumah and Patrice Lumumba.[23]

According to Joseph, the U.P.C. benefitted from the support of the southern Bamileke peasants and petty businessmen, while drawing tremendous support from the slums that the steel industries and sawmills in the Sanaga Maritime areas created around cities like Douala and New-Bell. The Sanaga Maritime provided one of the most enduring maquis for the guerilla wing of U.P.C.

The decision of the colonial government to ban this popular organization can be explained by the threat it posed for the declining French authority in the colonies. In 1954, the Vietminh defeated the French army; the outcome of this conflict was seen as a humiliation by French colonialism and as an encouraging victory for anticolonialist organizations in Africa. The same year, the war of liberation of Algeria was declared by the Front de Liberation Nationale. The fear of a third colonial war prompted the French strategists to use every means to liquidate genuine political developments in Cameroun.

The colonial government quickly sought to undermine the strength of the U.P.C. by intensifying the repression of a so-called "communist subversion": this was the excuse for all sorts of tricks, maneuvers of sabotage, and the creation as well as manipulations of conservative political parties in order to uproot and destroy the U.P.C. The final act of provocation took place on 22 May 1955, when the colonial police attacked U.P.C. members during a public meeting. It was immediately followed by the intervention of the French army and the burning down of U.P.C. headquarters, arrests, and the torture of people who were thought to be linked with the party. According to Abel Eyinga, it was estimated that between 2,000 and 2,500 people were killed during the tragic week starting on Monday, 22 May 1955.[24] The U.P.C. retaliated by cutting off electricity wires, roads, and railway lines at points connecting the Sanaga Maritime (where Ruben held his maquis) and Douala and Yaoundé (the stronghold of the colonial forces). The war went on until 1971, when the government caught and executed Ernest Ouandié, the last of the guerilla leaders still active in the country.

An interesting concordance emerges between the political and military program of the U.P.C. and the actions carried out by the Rubenist characters in Beti's Ruben novels at several levels, two of which are particularly striking. The report that Ruben was planning a government for the liberated zone of the country and his distrust for local chiefs who collaborated with the colonial power find a resounding echo in the novel *Lament for an African Pol* in the episode that describes the retreat of the Rubenists in the countryside during their march toward Ekoundoum. Their first and most important targets were the chief and the missionaries. Then, the Rubenists encouraged the formation of a village assembly responsible for law and justice. The revolutionary tribunal organized by the former "wives" of the chief stood for the new administrative body of the village. Could the concordance between these two spheres warrant the conclusion that the novels faithfully recreate the conditions of the war of liberation?

Such a conclusion would be erroneous, because the novel succeeds where the U.P.C. has failed. Creative imagination, it would appear, takes over at this point to pursue the quest and to bring the initiatory journey of Mor Zamba to a successful completion. However, the connection between the Ruben novels and the essay *Main basse sur le Cameroun* is acknowledged by the author himself. Beti's assessment of this connection invites the reader to see the Ruben trilogy as the novelistic version of the historical essay.

> Yes, it is true that there is a connection—in fact a close connection—between the fact that *Main basse sur le Cameroun* was seized and then banned and my sixth novel entitled *Remember Ruben* which, by the way, I started writing soon after the seizure . . . What I've just said is not only true for *Remember Ruben* but also for *Perpetua* and the novel I am currently serializing and which should be published in book form next year in March.[25] (My translation)

In their appreciation of the recent Camerounian past, serious historians of political life in Africa, like Joseph, generally distinguish between genuine political leaders, such as Ruben, and African civil servants, like Ahidjo, brought to power by the military might of the colonial government to whom they remain completely subservient in maintaining the neocolonial system in their countries. In his conclusion, Joseph registers the peculiar position of this repressive ruling class and wonders about its future.

> It remains to be seen which of the two main traditions in their modern political history the emerging Camerounian generation will

chose to honour: the glorious but only partly successful anti-colonial struggle of Ruben Um Nyobe, or the less glorious but more successful neo-colonial rule of Ahmadou Ahidjo.[26]

It is difficult to say what the choice of this generation will be, but it can be said that, at least since 1958, Beti has remained faithful to the ideals of Ruben despite the failure of U.P.C. to win the liberation war. The Ruben trilogy finds its origin in the circumstances indicated above. But it would be a serious mistake to equate the novels with the essay. Although Beti admits that there is a link between the two, he also warns against a reading that would ignore the fact that the novels are works of art where creative imagination plays a crucial role.[27]

The third major difference between the writers has to do with their personal experiences. Beti received his early education at Yaoundé, in his native Cameroun. It was during the years at the lycée that he discovered French literature, with writers such as Voltaire, whose *Candide* he appreciated, Montesquieu and his famous *Lettres Persanes*, and later on, Alexandre Dumas and his cyclical novels.[28] The author remembers that he received a "typical French school education" from the missionaries, and he admits that he has been unconsciously influenced by Voltaire's use of satire as a demystifying device. But Beti maintains that he did not like French literature in the way he was introduced to it, because—contrary to American literature—it generally appeared to be a bourgeois literature that often focused mainly on certain types of characters, intelligent and clean characters; as a high-school student, his dislike of the literature was compounded by the fact that he was forced to write essays on it. Regarding African writers, Beti shows a lot of admiration for the novelist Abdoulaye Sadji and the poet David Diop, but he finds Senghor and Ousmane Socé very conservative. His admiration for Sadji, who wrote two novels about women in a colonial society, may have influenced Beti to focus on the theme of women as victims in his novels, especially in *Perpetua*. Sadji's *Nini* and *Maïmouna* present female characters that are the victims of racism and African conservatism. Certainly Beti enjoyed reading Césaire and Damas but found little interest in the more conservative vein among Caribbean writers like René Maran, whose novel *Batouala* he condemns for painting an image of an acceptable colonialism. Thus, in African and Caribbean literatures, he finds two veins: the conservatives who try to accommodate the colonial regime by presenting a literature of exoticism, and those who are committed to the struggle of black peoples for freedom. This is Beti's favorite literature. Ironically, perhaps, he discovered these writers and trends, thanks to the *Anthologie de la nouvelle poésie nègre et malgache*, by Senghor.

During his formative years, Beti read two American writers who impressed him profoundly. At the lycée, he read Mark Twain's *Huckleberry Finn* and *Tom Sawyer*. Twain is a remarkable satirist and humorist—two devices that are important in Beti's writing—and his *King Leopold's Soliloquy* remains a landmark of anticolonialist vein in Western literature; it was published at a time when silence on the plight of the peoples of Africa was indeed the rule rather than the exception among American writers. The other American writer who influenced Beti in a very important way was Richard Wright, whose commitment to the struggle of the Afro-American people he found exemplary. Although he read Twain in Cameroun, he only discovered Wright in France. In "Le pauvre Christ de Bomba expliqué," Beti admires Richard Wright, whose actions "the fearful uncle Toms of the new black bourgeoisie" considered scandalous, and he sees in Wright "the first explosive prophet, at least in France, of the revolt of the ghettos" and, above all, "the indefatigable cicerone of their stupefying moral and material misery, the consequence of their oppression by the whites."[29] He urges all those interested in African literature to study the works of Richard Wright, "a black American writer who had an indisputable influence on the French public at the beginning of the fifties."

> The works of Richard Wright were not so much novels as the magic lantern which revealed the New World to the eager mind of a young African who had hardly disembarked from his colonial bush.[30] (My translation)

It is significant that later on Richard Wright traveled to Ghana and wrote a book titled *Black Power* on the first independent state in colonial Africa. The only other Afro-American writer Beti refers to is Chester Himes,[31] whose influence may be seen in his utilization of the investigative mode in *Perpetua*.

The discovery of Afro-American writers has been crucial for Beti. It was through the writings of Richard Wright that he became aware of the condition of Afro-Americans and of its similarity with the condition of the colonized Africans. It is remarkable that his political consciousness of the African predicament was mediated by his discovery of the historical condition of Afro-America. This is undoubtedly one of the reasons that explains the fact that Beti holds Wright as a kind of spiritual and ideological father; indeed, in political terms, he owes a part of his self-discovery to Richard Wright.[32] Finally, attention must be drawn to the admitted influence of Chinua Achebe's *Things Fall Apart* on Beti's use of language in order to reflect aspects of African speech patterns such as proverbs in his trilogy.[33]

Whereas Beti has lived in exile in France since 1959, Ngugi mainly lived in his native Kenya until the 1980s. His early formative years were spent at Kikuyu High School in Kenya during the Mau Mau war. From then on, he went to Makerere in Uganda in 1959 for undergraduate studies. At Makerere, he wrote his first short stories and two novels, *The River Between* and *Weep Not, Child*, in this order. He spent four years as a journalist in Nairobi before going to Leeds University for further studies. According to Bernth Lindfors,

> Between May 1961 and August 1964 Ngugi wrote nearly eighty pieces for the Nairobi press, contributing first to the *Sunday Post*, then preparing a fairly regular weekly or fortnightly column for the

> *Sunday Nation*, and finally working full time as a "Junior Reporter" and editorial commentator for the *Daily Nation* in the months between his graduation from Makerere and his departure for post graduate studies at Leeds University in England.[34]

Beti also spent a few years in journalism. Although I was unable to recover more than two essays that he published in *Preuves* in 1958 and 1959, Gerald Moore and Eloise A. Brière report that he also wrote articles for *La Revue Camerounaise*. It is in the 1958 article that Beti disclosed the death of Ruben Um Nyobe.[35]

If journalism is an experience shared by the two writers, they differ in their readings and the authors who impressed them. For instance, the influence of Joseph Conrad's *Under Western Eyes* on Ngugi's *A Grain of Wheat* has been vigorously and meticulously argued by various critics. But, in general, the same critics fail to note the ideological influence of Fanon's *The Wretched of the Earth* on the writings of Ngugi. According to Peter Nazareth,

> A few weeks before Ngugi started work on his novel, he came across the work of Frantz Fanon, thanks to Grant Kamenju who had picked up a copy of Fanon's *The Damned* (now entitled *The Wretched of the Earth*) in Paris.[36]

Since at least 1969, Ngugi has consistently quoted Fanon in his numerous essays. In a sense, *The Wretched of the Earth* is his bible. Another writer who may have had an impact on Ngugi is the Caribbean novelist George Lamming, on whose novel *In The Castle of My Skin* Ngugi wrote one of his most insightful essays of literary criticism. Yet no writer has exercised as strong an attraction on Ngugi as Sembène Ousmane, for even while in detention, Sembène is among Ngugi's all-time favorite authors. Ngugi goes as far as quoting *God's Bits of Wood* with admiration within the very pages of his own novel *Petals of Blood*. With Sembène, Ngugi has found a stylistic and ideological brotherhood. Both writers are avowed socialists, both consistently use sequences of scenes in a cinematic fashion in their novels, and both writers received the remarkable Lotus Prize for Afro-Asian Literature in 1973.[37] Ngugi has also joined and then gone further than Sembène in the campaign in favor of writing in African languages.

Although their readings indicate different influences,[38] Beti and Ngugi have equally suffered from censorship for their political ideas, and while Beti has lived in exile since 1959, Ngugi has recently been forced into exile following his release from detention.

It appears then that despite the personal,[39] linguistic, and historical differences between these two writers and their countries' past and present histories, their study belongs to an important phase in the history of African literatures, a phase of visionary novelists; the exploration of historical and visionary sensibilities in their works is both a mode of self-apprehension and the portrayal of a greater movement in society toward a new cultural and political awareness.

The organization of this essay follows a simple plan. After this chapter, which examines the intellectual and social milieu that informs the creative work of the two writers, the next chapter is devoted to a study of the role and function of myths in their novels. Two more chapters are subsequently devoted to a study of the historical vision that emerges from the works as a totality, and chapter five examines the stylistic innovations that exist in the narratives. The conclusion summarizes the findings of the study and restates the case (first made in chapter two) for the mythopoeic trend to be seen as a powerful stylized statement of a new cultural awareness.

Notes 1

[1] Except in Gerald Moore, *Twelve African Writers* (Bloomington: Indiana University Press, 1980), and Bernard Mouralis, *L'oeuvre de Mongo Beti* (Paris: Editions Saint Paul, 1981), this aspect of the novels has received very little attention.

[2] The novels under study as the Ruben trilogy are Mongo Beti, *Remember Ruben* (London: Heinemann, 1980) [hereafter referred to as *Ruben*], *Perpetua and the Habit of Unhappiness* (London: Heinemann, 1978) [hereafter referred to as *Perpetua*], and *Lament for an African Pol* (Washington, D. C.: Three Continents Press, 1985) [hereafter referred to as *Lament*].

The novels under study as the Mau Mau trilogy are Ngugi wa Thiong'o, *Weep Not, Child* (New York: Macmillan, 1969) [hereafter referred to as *Weep Not*], *A Grain of Wheat* (London: Heinemann, 1971) [hereafter referred to as *Grain*], and *Petals of Blood* (New York: E. P. Dutton, 1977) [hereafter referred to as *Petals*]. All subsequent references to the novels of the trilogies refer to the above editions.

[3] Eza Boto [Mongo Beti], "Sans haine et sans amour," *Présence Africaine*, nos. 14-15 (June-September 1953): 213-20.

[4] "An Interview with Ngugi," *The Weekly Review* (Nairobi), 9 January 1978, 10.

[5] Gilbert Durand, *Les Structures anthropologiques de l'imaginaire* (Paris: Bordas, 1969), 64: "Nous entendons par mythe un système dynamique de symboles, d'archétypes et de shèmes, système dynamique qui, sous l'impulsion d'un système, tend à se composer en récit. Le mythe est déja une esquisse de rationalisation puisqu'il utilise le fil du discours dans lequel les symboles se résolvent en mots et les archétypes en idées . . . le mythe promeut . . . le récit historique et légendaire."

[6] Jean-Pierre Salgas, "Aimé Césaire, le poète en quête d'histoire," *Jeune Afrique*, no. 1142 (November 1982): 74.

[7] Edward Baugh, "The West Indian Writer and His Quarrel with History," *Tapia* 7, no. 8 (1977): 6-7; and *Tapia* 8, no. 9 (1977): 6-7, 11.

[8] For example, *Remember Ruben* for the main part is set in colonial Africa, but the dedication immediately establishes a corrolation with neocolonial Africa. It was dedicated to Blondin Diop, a young Senegalese social critic and political activist who died in prison in Senegal. The Government of Léopold S. Senghor alleged that he committed suicide, but many African observers remain skeptical about this official statement. The news of the death of Blondin Diop sparked public indignation and ignited violent student protests throughout Senegal.

Although *Remember Ruben* was never banned in Senegal, it is rumored that many bookstores sold the novel with the dedication page removed, presumably on orders from government officials who feared that it would rekindle public anger at the circumstances under which Blondin Diop died. In effect, the sentiment expressed in the dedication remains very clear:

> To Diop Blondin, proud son of Africa, my young brother,
> murdered in the foul prisons of an African ruler.
> Africa, harsh mother, forever fertile in mercenary tyrants!

[9] Claude Meillassoux, "Le mâle en gésine ou De l'historicité des mythes," *Cahiers d'Etudes Africaines*, nos. 73-76 (1979): 353-80.

[10] Ngugi wa Thiong'o and Ngugi wa Miiri, *Ngaahika Ndenda*, (London: Heinemann Educational Books [East Africa], 1980); trans. Ngugi wa Thiong'o and Ngugi wa Miiri, *I Will Marry When I Want* (London: Heinemann African Writers Series, 1982).

[11] Ngugi wa Thiong'o, *Caitaani Mutharabi-ini* (Nairobi: Heinemann, 1980); English translation, *Devil on the Cross* (London: Heinemann, 1982). In his recent book of essays, *Decolonizing the Mind* (London: Heinemann, 1986), Ngugi says that this book stands for his "farewell to English as the vehicle of my writing."

[12] Mongo Beti, "Les langues africaines et l'impérialisme culturel français," *Peuples Noirs/Peuples Africains*, no. 29 (September-October 1982): 106-18.

[13] Karim Traoré and Jean-Claude Naba, "Y'a bon français africain," *Peuples Noirs/Peuples Africains*, no. 32 (March-April 1983): 15-27.

[14] Although Ngugi may have read English translations of novels by Mongo Beti, the latter had read nothing by Ngugi in 1981 (personal interview, April 1981), despite their common interest in the Mau Mau revolution.

[15] George Padmore, *Pan-africanism or communism* (London: Denis Dobson, 1956), 211. See also, Donald Barnett and Njama Karari, *Mau Mau from Within* (New York: Monthly Review Press, 1966).

[16] Ngugi's family lived as squatters (*ahoy*): "As a boy, I used to pick pyrenthum flowers for one of the very few African landlords in pre-independence Limuru. The landlord on whose land we lived as 'ahoy' had an orchard of pears and plums." See Ngugi wa Thiong'o, *Detained: A Writer's Prison Diary* (London: Heinemann, 1981), 106.

[17] Ibid., 82.

[18] Mbiyu Koinange, *The People of Kenya Speak for Themselves* (Detroit: Kenya Publication Fund, 1955), 25-48.

[19] Ngugi, *Detained*, 86: "The Kenyatta of the 1930's was talking about the inevitable collapse of the old British Empire, falling to the united blows of its enslaved workers and peasants. Yes, Kenyatta was talking about a liberated Kenya, concretely meaning the liberation of all the workers and peasants of all Kenyan nationalities from the imperialist economic exploitation and political and cultural oppression. More, he was talking of a free Africa—in 1933. This was the Kenyatta of 'the burning spear,' of whom the Kenyan masses then rightly sang as their coming saviour. This was the Kenyatta reflected in my novel, *Weep Not, Child*, about whom the peasant characters whispered at night."

[20] Ibid., 82.

[21] Richard A. Joseph, "Ruben Um Nyobe and the 'Kamerun' Rebellion," *African Affairs* 73, no. 293 (1974): 430. For further studies on Cameroun, see also David Kom, *Le Cameroun* (Paris: Editions Sociales, 1971); Abel Eyinga, *Mandat d'arrêt pour cause d'élections* (Paris: L'Harmattan, 1978); Georges Chaffard, *Carnets Secrets de la décolonisation*, vol. 2 (Paris: Calmann-Levy, 1968); Richard A. Joseph, *Radical Nationalism in Cameroun* (London: Clarendon Press, 1977); and J. A. Mbembe, ed., *Ruben Um Nyobe, Le problème national Kamerunais* (Paris: L'Harmattan, 1984).

[22] Mongo Beti, *Main basse sur le Cameroun* (Paris: Maspero, 1972).

[23] Joseph, "Ruben Um Nyobe," 430.

[24] Abel Eyinga, *Introduction à la politique Camerounaise* (Paris: Editions Anthropos, 1978), 85.

[25] Anthony Biakolo, "Entretien avec Mongo Beti," *Peuples Noirs/Peuples Africains*, no. 10 (July-August 1979): 104-105: "Oui, il est vrai qu'il y a un lien—même un lien étroit—entre le fait qu'on m'a saisi et interdit ensuite un livre qui s'appelle *Main basse sur le Cameroun* et mon sixième roman qui s'appelle *Remember Ruben* que j'ai commencé aussitôt d'ailleurs après cette saisie. . . . Ce que je viens de dire n'est pas seulement vrai pour *Remember Ruben* mais aussi pour *Perpétue* et pour le roman que je publie actuellement en feuilleton et qui paraitra en volume l'année prochaine au mois de mars (1979)." The novel that is alluded to is *Lament*.

[26] Joseph, "Ruben Um Nyobe," 448.

[27] Biakolo, "Entretien," 106.

[28] Roger Mercier, M. Battestini, and S. Battestini, *Mongo Beti, écrivain Camerounais; Textes commentés* (Paris: Fernand Nathan, 1964). In his introduction, Mercier reports that Beti envisioned writing an essay on the novels of Alexandre Dumas. This report is the first indication of Beti's interest in the cyclical novel such as the Ruben novels.

[29] Mongo Beti, "Le pauvre Christ de Bomba expliqué," *Peuples Noirs/Peuples Africains*, no. 19 (January-February 1981): 104-32.

[30] Ibid., 116: "Les oeuvres de Richard Wright furent moins des romans que la lanterne magique jetant le Nouveau Monde en pature à l'avidité d'un petit Africain à peine débarqué de sa brousse coloniale."

[31] Chester Himes became very famous in France as a master of the detective novel. For a study of Himes's novels, see Ambroise Kom, *Le Harlem de Chester Himes* (Sherbrooke, Quebec: Editions Naaman, 1978), and F. Stephen Milliken, *Chester Himes: A Critical Approach* (Columbia: University of Missouri Press, 1976).

[32] Beti, "Le pauvre Christ," 119.

[33] Biakolo, "Entretien," 114.

[34] Bernth Lindfors, "Ngugi wa Thiong'o's Early Journalism" (Paper presented at the African Studies Association Annual Conference, Los Angeles, Calif., 1978), 2.

[35] Mongo Beti, "Lettre de Yaoundé: Cameroun 1958," *Preuves*, no. 94 (December 1958): 56, and "Tumultueux Cameroun," *Preuves*, no. 103 (September 1959): 30-39.

[36] Peter Nazareth, *Literature and Society in Modern Africa* (Nairobi: East African Literature Bureau, 1972), 128. This piece of information is confirmed by Ime Ikkideh in his preface to Ngugi's *Homecoming* (New York: Lawrence Hill and Company, 1973), xiii.

[37] See "Special Section on *Lotus* Laureates for the Year 1973," *Lotus,* no. 19 (1974). This issue carries a short story by James Ngugi (Ngugi wa Thiong'o), "The Return," 173-83, (and its French translation) and this appreciation: "This authentic writer has taken interest in the cause of his people, the conflicts in his community and in Africa in general. He has devoted all his time and efforts to these issues. Therefore, he has been deservedly awarded the Lotus Prize for Afro-Asian literature for 1973, in recognition of his person and in appreciation of his literary creation" (p. 177).

[38] The literary influence shared by these two novelists is orature. Mongo Beti has already indicated his early interest in Mvet narrative. (See Mercier, Battestini, and Battestini, *Mongo Beti*.) And in *Decolonizing the Mind*, 71-72, Ngugi writes about the earliest literary influences he received: "As I have explained I grew up speaking Gikuyu. My first encounter with stories and oral narratives was through Gikuyu. As a new literate in Gikuyu, I avidly read the bible, particularly the stories in the Old Testament."

[39] Another difference—but of a lesser consequence for this study—between these two novelists is their views on religion. Ngugi was raised a Christian, but like many Africans, he abandoned his Christian name. He admits to having been influenced by the Old Testament. This biblical influence is noted in Ngugi's novels by various critics. Beti was noted for his criticism of missionaries in Africa, particularly the use of religion for material and political gains as it implies exploitation of others. He is an avowed agnostic. Nevertheless, religious sentiment is always present in their novels.

2

Novels as Dramatization of History
Elements of the Mythic and Epic Background in the Trilogies

Elements of the Mythic and Epic Background in *Remember Ruben*

The Spirit of Akomo Betrayed

Seen together, the novels that form Mongo Beti's Ruben trilogy convey the sense of an epic sweep materialized by their extension in time and space. The first novel, *Remember Ruben*, starts with a problem of genesis. Mor-Zamba, the hero of the novel, is a foundling. Nobody could tell which family he belonged to, hence his name, which means "Providential Man" in Beti language. His quest for identity through the history of the Camerounian people is partially satisfied when, at the end of the novel, he learns from his friend Abena that he is the grandson of the late chief of Ekoundoum. He then decides to return to Ekoundoum to fight the despot chief; the story of his return is told in *Lament*. *Remember Ruben* covers some forty years of the history of Cameroun, through World War II to independence in 1960.

Perpetua, the second novel, continues the story to the 1970s. The novel takes the form of an investigation into the causes of Perpetua's death. The investigation is conducted by her brother, Essola, a former militant of the P. P. P. (the fictionalized name of the historic U. P. C., the political party headed by the nationalist leader Ruben Um Nyobe, whose name provides the title for two of Beti's novels). After serving a long jail-term in the prisons of the dictator Baba Toura, Essola is released with the provision that he join the dictator's party.

Although *Lament* is a sequel of the first novel, it does not deal with the time of Mor-Zamba's childhood. It focuses on the first years of independence, depicting a Cameroun caught in a total state of anarchy and violence. By responding to the popular call from Ekoundoum, Mor-Zamba acquires the ultimate characteristic of the epic hero. By liberating the people of Ekoundoum from a despotic chief, he regains his full identity and returns to the community.

One of the pillars that sustain epic action is the reliance on myth as the leading light in the grand time swing proper to the epic narrative. *Remember Ruben* is an epic narrative both by the life it describes and the style in which it is depicted. Time, as we shall see, is limitless, inexhaustible, and dense. The plot freely multiplies itself, creating subplots born out of each other and resulting in an illusion of endlessness, through a psychological intensity that derives from the intensity of the life thus portrayed. Epic action develops in epic time; the action often plunges into the remote past, the apprehension of which is sometimes made possible through a name, a character who is both remote and close, and whose unmediated presence seems totally overwhelming. That character, whose existence finds a place in countless stories illustrating every moment in the life of the community, is the link that bridges the gulf between history and the unfathomable time of origins.

While setting up the framework of the epic story, the narrator of *Remember Ruben* appeals to Akomo, the ancestral creator of the Essazam nation; by doing so he conjures up the most fundamental pillar of the community and, by the same token, brings forth a time span of unlimited extent. A careful reading will show that all the elements proper to the epic form the foundations of this narrative. These elements include a mystic reference, the characterization proper to the epic hero, and divine presence often expressed in prophetic terms throughout the narrative. It will also appear to the reader that all these three major elements that set the tone for epic action are structurally interrelated in the dynamic progression of the novel.

Mythic Reference and Divine Presence

The principal mythic reference in *Remember Ruben* is a myth of origin that relates to Akomo, the founder of the Essazam nation. The narrator summons his spirit by calling his name in situations where the community's behavior undergoes judgment, and—we shall see why—compares Mor-Zamba to Akomo because the latter's action, it is presumed, represents standard social behavior. In other words, a reference to Akomo is an attempt to discover the ideal solution to a problem; hence, the structural connection between Akomo and the epic hero is, within the narrative, a functional relationship. The presence of the mythical ancestor is basically a normative presence, the musical tone that modulates the course of the action to be carried out. The carriers of such action, when faced with countless obstacles, seem to enjoy the intervention of a superior hand guiding them, though they may not even be conscious of it. Although they make errors, they swear by principles that, the narrator claims, have been laid out as a result of Akomo's life experience. Since Akomo's life experience, endless as it were, incorporates all the values of the Essazam, it then becomes clear that these values represent the higher qualities to which each member of the clan aspires. In other words, these values represent the totality of the clan's values at the very moment when the heroes of the narrative seek to conquer or reconquer them.

Although the founder's name does not appear until the second chapter of the novel, it is subtly announced by references to a divine presence. Thus, at the very beginning of the story, the narrator offers a prelude of the action to come. This prelude brings Mor-Zamba, a child, a foundling, face to face with Engamba, a mean old man, in a clash at dawn. Engamba accuses the little orphan of stealing oranges when he could have had a hot meal had he only asked for it. His excessive anger at the child's refusal to follow him is beyond reason. Easily recognizable in the confrontation are two familiar characters in West African tales: the mean, ugly, and hypocritical hyena versus the little, weak, and clever hare. We can also identify the humorous caricature of the wrong and the right, the criminal and the victim, the terrorist and the terrorized child, both standing in a David-and-Goliath posture by the road at dawn. Having presented the situation, and the origin of Engamba's quarrel, the narrator of *Remember Ruben*, acting as the judge of the conflict, summons "Providence" or "Heaven" to his help. Remembering the past, he states,

> True, the young traveler did help himself at the orange-tree growing on the clan lands; but, according to tradition, such a tree doesn't belong any more to the occupants than to the passers-by who, as necessity demands, may enjoy it as liberally as the water of the stream, the freshness of the forest shade, or any other blessing furnished by *Providence*. No one had planted that orange-tree, so far as we could remember; no one claimed to be the owner. (*Ruben*, p. 4; my emphasis)

Thus, the defense of Mor-Zamba, the wandering child, is that Providence is on his side because it represents Truth, and Truthful Providence is Rightful Providence. After all, isn't Mor-Zamba a child of unknown origins? The old man who adopts him is convinced that in addition to his mysterious origin, Mor-Zamba

> was a victim of a mysterious sickness: he was either deaf or dumb; or both at the same time. *Heaven* itself had directed him to stop at Ekoundoum, just as bush animals sometimes approach the abode of men, when the pain and misery of their sickness makes them search for care. (*Ruben*, p. 10; my emphasis)

In both these excerpts, the narrator uses the terms "Heaven" and "Providence" in connection with Mor-Zamba's meeting of the clan of Ekoundoum through the mediation of two elders of the city: the hostile Engamba and the nameless, yet hospitable, old man who is simply referred to as "the wise old man" or "the old man." It appears that this namelessness, reminiscent of the creator's in the early stages of the narrative, is important in conferring upon the old man the status of a prophet.

The creator's name, however, is mentioned several times as the story proceeds. It is useful to note that the narrator mentions Akomo while Mor-Zamba is being persecuted as the collective scapegoat of the citizens of Ekoundoum. Their intolerance of Mor-Zamba's presence in the city turns Engamba and his gang of hypocrites into fanatics.

Undoubtedly, the narrative hook consists here in isolating the name Akomo, thus leading us to the last paragraph of the chapter for a concise description of the character. The final sentence of the paragraph once more subtly links Akomo to Mor-Zamba by a rhetorical question.

> The bards with their sweet instruments, those experts in all the exploits of Akomo, offered us different versions about the origins of the hero who had founded our ancient race. Some said he came from a tree; others from the snake of the great river which divides the shores of life and death; others declared they didn't know where he sprang from, having suddenly appeared among us, a young man huge, strong and beautiful, with a voice of thunder, a martial and noble stride, a brow furrowed with lightning, an open heart. *Yet who would take refuge in Akomo's doubtful origin, in order to refuse him his homage?* (Ruben, pp. 22-23; my emphasis)

In this question, there is a hardly veiled allusion to Mor-Zamba as a descendant, perhaps a human replica, of Akomo. In any case, the similarity between them is all too clear to leave any doubt that those who seek to drive Mor-Zamba out of the city on the basis of his unknown origins are criminals in the traditions of the community. Although Mor-Zamba is continually mistreated, Akomo is not mentioned by name again until the end of the third chapter, when at the end of a dinner, Abena attacks the youth of the city as a bunch of hypocrites. The old man tells the assembled youth a didactic tale based on Akomo's experience among giants as a warning against failing to live up to their traditions. After this short reference to Akomo, the creator of the Essazam nation is seldom mentioned by name; more and more the narrator refers to him as "Providence" or "Heaven."

The mythic reference in its divine character is brought into the story by little drops of details in the manner of a pointillistic picture. In the first chapter, the narrator uses the words "Providence" and "Heaven." It is not until the second chapter that the name of Akomo is mentioned, although it is isolated and unqualified as if the audience of the narrator knew the character. The end of chapter two identifies the name of Akomo with the founding of "the race" while describing him succinctly. Akomo appears again in the third paragraph as a behavioral standard in the aforementioned story.

This pointillistic introduction of Akomo into the story is consistent with the general modulation of the narrative itself. In this book, each major part of the plot is dominated by a mythic figure, be it Akomo, Ruben, or Abena. Except for Abena, their names disappear from the text of the second Ruben novel (*Lament*), when the decisive battle is engaged in the city of Ekoundoum. At this point, Abena survives through the freedom fighters and through the good mother Ngwane-Eligui The Elder, who is his mother as well as the adoptive mother of Mor-Zamba.

For the moment, let it suffice to point out the musical function of modulator played by the mythic reference Akomo. As Durand suggests, myth tends to repeat a theme as does music.[1] The myth of Akomo stresses at the societal level the ideals and aspirations of the Essazam that in turn are going to be unraveled by the narrator of the Ruben novels in different settings, at different times within different social relationships, as the struggle for justice continues.

The Epic Hero as a Human Replica of Akomo

The role that Akomo, the mythic reference, plays in the prelude of the narrative also serves as the model for the hero of the epic story. As pointed out, Mor-Zamba is subtly likened to Akomo, the mythic creator of the Essazam nation. When the narrator asks, "Who would take refuge in Akomo's doubtful origin to refuse him his homage?" he suggests that Mor-Zamba deserves the same treatment as Akomo (*Ruben*, p. 23). Furthermore, the question follows a description of Akomo, whose origins, we are told, are as mysterious as Mor-Zamba's. Akomo is described as a strong noble man endowed with a great heart. In the narrative, this characterization of the creator is enlarged into Mor-Zamba as a heroic character; here, mythical traits find their concrete expression in context. Using superlatives, the narrator describes Mor-Zamba as a particularly gifted young man.

The orphan child has the highest physical qualities among children of his age. He also appears to be the most giving of all; helping anyone who requests his aid. Although he gives without asking for anything in return, he not only makes enemies for daring to rest (the old woman Mbolo accuses him of laziness), but receives no help while building his house. Mor-Zamba and Abena build an entire house on their own. Although they enjoy the expertise and guidance of the old man, nobody else is willing to help them gather the material necessary for the construction. Having built the house all by themselves—a task customarily accomplished by a whole team of young men, often assisted by young women—Mor-Zamba and Abena have become celebrated as an exceptional duo in the slogan, "When Abena and Mor-Zamba are leagued together, what mountains can they not move?" (*Ruben*, p. 26).

Furthermore, Mor-Zamba's courage and determination in life remain unparalleled in the narrative. This particular aspect of the character appears in his long apprenticeship as a truck driver in Kola-Kola, in his confrontations with the police in Oyolo, as well as in his tour de force in saving the life of Ruben nearly at the cost of his own. Even in Camp Gouverneur Leclerc, a notorious forced labor camp, his kindness and compassion have no limit.

If Mor-Zamba's description is based on a sketch of Akomo, his formative years are those of a disinherited prince, alienated from his people and the power his father once held. The numerous difficulties he encounters during his quest appear to be the classical obstacles that emerge on the itinerary of the epic hero. To begin with, Mor-Zamba's appearance in Ekoundoum is comparable to a rebirth. It bears a striking resemblance to the Biblical story of the Messiah, but beyond that is the overwhelming observation that in most epic narratives the hero's origin appears problematic.

Mor-Zamba appeared in the city as an orphan. The theme of orphanhood is quite common in African tales, and it has been used by many contemporary African writers, including Camerounian novelists. Such orphan tales are characterized by a quest in the form of a journey made impossible by countless obstacles that mushroom on the road taken by the orphan. However the orphan always encounters a special character—an old woman, an old man, a childlike figure, or sometimes an animal or a tree— who offers the child invaluable guidance. The quest of the orphan, like the quest in general within African narratives, is patterned after initiation processes into manhood or womanhood. And it appears that in the folk tales the quest is often successful, indicating the full completion of the initiation of the hero.[2]

In his first novel, *Ville cruelle*, Beti tells the story of Banda, a young man who grows up suffering from the absence of his deceased father. In *Le pauvre Christ de Bomba*, Denis is an orphan child whose quest fails, much like Banda's. It appears that the failure in these orphan children's education is due to the alienating character of the colonial situation.

In *Remember Ruben*, Beti carries this technique to its full completion; the orphan's quest leads him to maturity. In the folk tale, the successful orphan is usually rewarded for his perseverance in intelligently undoing traps or by passing obstacles during his initiatory journey; he receives a fabulous material wealth or, more often, appears extraordinarily wise. This successful quest is completed in what we may call "the *Remember Ruben* cycle." Mor-Zamba is an orphan found at a crossroad on the outskirts of the city. He is typically hungry and dressed in threadbare clothes. The narrator metaphorically describes him as an animal to signify his love for freedom and his closeness to nature as well as, by implication, his leery attitude to society as a being deliberately kept on the margin of mainstream Ekoundoum.

Mor-Zamba is, however, an unusual orphan. Isidore Okpewho observes that "there is something in the birth and early youth of the hero that sets him apart from the natural course of life."[3] Like Sunjata, who was born a cripple, Mor-Zamba strikes the people of Ekoundoum as a mute and deaf child. This physical disability, if nothing else, sets him apart from the other children of the city. Mor-Zamba's muteness and deafness symbolize his state of infancy, of newbornness in terms of society. His inability to communicate in society cripples him. Mor-Zamba must seek the usage of language. Another mythical element present in the story is reminiscent of a biblical story. It is clear that the great majority of Ekoundoum is hostile to the orphan child. In addition to Engamba's personal anger at the child, the entire city seems to be at odds with Mor-Zamba. For the first time, the Essazam are undergoing a clinical case of xenophobia, and like the people of Christ, Ekoundoum decided to cast stones at one of its own children. Despite the fact that Mor-Zamba is adopted by an elder of the city, the children of Ekoundoum, led by Engamba's son, break the sanctity of the good elder's home and proceed to terrify and persecute the innocent orphan even while he is eating his first hot meal in a long time.

In the light of the events unraveled by the narrator, it is appropriate to see Mor-Zamba as being born in Ekoundoum. It is in Ekoundoum that he recovers the use of speech, is given a name, raised, and nearly married, without ever being accepted by the people of the city. Apart from the old man, Abena, and his mother, the birth of Mor-Zamba only attracts the curious, the talkative, and the generally hostile people led by Engamba.

> The news of the event, which at first had affected only those parts of the city nearest to the road, now spread into the remotest quarters, and even into the bush beyond. Like pilgrims flocking to adore an image, they came in long processions, at once fervent, happy and sacrilegious, to tramp through the old man's house or, once it was full, to gather all around it, eager to catch a glimpse of this new marvel, a wandering and solitary child. (*Ruben*, p. 12)

The origins of Mor-Zamba are revealed at the end of *Remember Ruben*. In reality, the foundling is the direct grandson of the legitimate chief of Ekoundoum, who died in mysterious circumstances and whose family was thereafter deliberately scattered away from the city. As the grandson of the former chief of the city, Mor-Zamba is not only a legitimate citizen, but also a claimant to political office. It should be noted that the theme of orphanhood deepens when the narrator reveals that Mor-Zamba's mother was also an orphan.

In reference to the question of the origins of the hero, Okpewho makes the following observation:

> the hero of the (epic) song usually has the advantages of birth that set him above the rank and file. Sunjata is the son of a king and later himself a *mansa* (emperor). His mother, Sogolon (Sukulung), is the "buffalo woman" and then brings to the hero all the mystic force of her totemic personality . . . Silamaka of the *Silamaka* epic is the son of the chief of Macina. Ozidi is of the ruling house of Orua—his father is killed by fellow townsmen and

his entire career builds up to his absolute sovereignty. The hero of the *Kambili* epic is the son of Kanji, a general of the emperor Samory Touré . . . Mwindo of *The Mwindo Epic* is the son of Tubondo.[4]

In epic stories, the hero indeed has outstanding origins. Although the hero may be of an extraordinary descent, that does not confer upon him the distinction of hero; on the contrary, it may be the source of his difficulties. In any case, it appears that he must lose all socially inherited privileges and seek to regain his humanity through an unusually terrifying number of obstacles. The hero starts out with the bare minimum, or even worse, without support. He is an oppressed child, lives a depressed adolescence, and as he enters adult society, begins to make slow and painful accomplishments. What sustains the action and secures the attention of the audience is a line of victories that pearl the growth of the character. Physical handicaps, poverty, and other temporary physical and moral disabilities are overcome. Yet, the greatest and most encouraging victory of the disinherited child is his ability to survive.

It has been implied that there is something admirable embedded in the origin of the child. On the contrary, it is because the hero is socially the ultimate orphan that he must struggle harder than all. When he finally regains what some have always enjoyed by birthright, no one disputes the validity of his achievements, and the place he secures for himself and for the entire community is the ultimate goal of his quest and the measure of his greatness.

Prophetic Statements

The social birth of Mor-Zamba, the narrator of *Remember Ruben* tells us, seems to indicate the beginning of troubles for Ekoundoum. As Okpewho puts it, "the advent of the hero in the world is marked by some awe or mystery; some portentous event."[5] In chapter four, part one, the narrator tells us that the arrival of Mor-Zamba in the city has coincided with the beginning of a rather bleak period in the history of Ekoundoum. It seems as if Providence had elected to send premonitory signs to those who had abandoned the principles of Akomo and "the ancestral cult" for their own extravagance and greedy appetites.

> Mor-Zamba marked for our city the beginning of a curse, after which everything seemed stranger, or should I say sadder, more disquieting, more hostile perhaps; in any case, more bitter, as if some malevolent pressure had squeezed all the juice of life towards the future, condemning us henceforth to an uncertain and exasperating expectation. As for this future it looked very far off to us, like a country in which we could only arrive, if we ever did, by crossing many perilous rivers and fighting with enemies of every sort; or rather, it threatened to reveal itself momentarily, like an equivocal dream; one of those visions which mingle intuitions of horror with splendours of ineffable beauty. (*Ruben*, pp. 31-32)

In portraying this difficult future for the community, the narrator also functions as a prophet. Epic narratives often include prophecies as a structural device in the development of the story. In *Sundiata*, in *Kambili*, and in *The Mwindo Epic*,[6] the narrative line is constantly sustained by prophecies. These prophecies are sometimes found in the mouth of a child, in the words of the narrator, or, more often, in the statements of an elderly character. In *Remember Ruben*, the wise elder who adopts Mor-Zamba plays the role of the prophet.

When Mor-Zamba narrowly escapes death by drowning at the hands of Engamba's son, the narrator's description of the old man gives us a sense of the importance of the event and the message he wants to deliver to Ekoundoum. The old man is seen as a voice coming out of the darkness, thus losing his former identity of a flesh and blood creature to become the divine messenger.

> He waited till nightfall . . . then he posted himself in the middle of the road adjoining the roadway, blew a long blast on his horn to draw attention, and announced in a voice all the more impressive in that it came from the darkness and bore the accent of Justice on the heels of Crime. (*Ruben*, p. 17)

The immediate act of purification that the words of the prophet give occasion to only provides temporary relief for Mor-Zamba from the hostility of Ekoundoum. When, against all rules, Engamba refuses to marry his daughter to Mor-Zamba, the prophet once again emerges in the old man ; angered by the hypocrisy of the elders who support Engamba, the old man consults the oracles. The result of his test is clear; the council of elders has transgressed the sacred tradition of the community. This time, the prophet curses the city.

> Justice has well and truly been injured, and Providence, consulted by us, announces a coming misfortune through the voices of these birds. The clan has violated a sacred law and will be well punished for it; I shall rejoin them tomorrow and tell them: "Your cowardice, together with the pride and egotism of Engamba, have unloosed the bonds of disaster; it glides even now over our heads; it will swoop at any moment. . ." (*Ruben*, p. 59)

Another premonitory sign associated with prophecies is found in the presence of animals. In *Remember Ruben*, the gods who are betrayed manifest the omen all night through a concert of owls.

The old man's prophecy and curse quickly manifest themselves in the precipitous departure of visitors from the city, his sudden death soon thereafter, and the kidnapping of Mor-Zamba for forced labor. The kidnapping of Mor-Zamba by the colonial troops triggers Abena's departure, and it seems as if the best citizens of Ekoundoum leave the city in order to escape imminent catastrophes. As part one of the novel ends, the narrator remembers the woes that were to befall the city.

> Thus it was that in the space of a season, unless we no longer remember the matter exactly, our city lost its two greatest hearts; its soul, one might say. We didn't realize it at once, but this was a wound which would never really close again. For the next twenty years we were to be sapped by all kinds of vexations, like those experienced, perhaps, by the newly-born, thrust suddenly from the warm and palpitating womb which shadows them, crucified by the harsh light of day, deafened by the cacophony of life, shaken by the freezing vibrations of the air. (*Ruben,* p. 64)

Once again the narrator compares Mor-Zamba to Akomo, but this time he associates Abena to the comparison. When Abena and Mor-Zamba leave Ekoundoum, the narrator utters the name Akomo for the last time, as if to bless the two companions.

> We had to wait these same twenty years to learn, little by little, of the odyssey worthy of Akomo himself, lived by the two most admirable sons of Ekoundoum. (*Ruben*, pp. 64-65)

Thus, all references to Akomo cease as the narrative flows outside of the confines of Ekoundoum toward the colonial city.

Conclusion

It is useful to point out the narrator's use of the word "odyssey" as a signal to the reader. This invitation to read *Remember Ruben* as an epic story is justified in the text by the presence of various elements used in a manner proper to the epic narrative. The narrative uses a myth of origin as the basis of the story. It also depicts a character whose heroic actions are likened to the deeds of the mythical creator of the Essazam nation. I have tried to show how much the development of the narrative itself depends on the simple, yet revealing, use of prophetic statements that allow the narrator to outline future developments in the life of Ekoundoum, thus becoming a major narrative technique.

Elements of the Mythic and Epic Background in *Weep Not, Child*

The works of Ngugi display a significant use of myths. They are utilized, structurally, as a support canvas for the epic action that spans his trilogy of Kenya. His novels (*Weep Not, Child, A Grain of Wheat,* and *Petals of Blood*) are set within the context of social crises in the history of Kenya. The first two novels are set within the context of the Emergency, also known as the Mau Mau uprising, which set the Land and Freedom Army against the British colonial army, from 1952 to 1958. As for *Petals of Blood*, it is set in the decade or so that followed Kenya's successful struggle for self-rule.

In order to appreciate the epic quality of the novels, it is necessary to read them as one long narrative. This prescription arises out of the established link between the three works in the broad historical, social, and geographic context that they share. Moreover, all three books focus on the Mau Mau uprising and its impact on individuals as well as on Kenyan society. The narrative as a whole, however, is more ambitious than a simple description of social crises. It dramatizes the spirit of a people through their history in order to arrive at and dwell on some particular moments—turning points, as it were—in their quest for freedom.

This giant scope, the scope of an epic narrative, is the scope of *Weep Not, Child*. It could easily get out of hand if it were to be contained in such a short novel. It would be, one might say, too loaded, too heavy a novel—one that evokes the spirit of an epic story without embracing the totality of its cosmological, all-encompassing quality. Indeed, Gerald Moore has indicated that "In this novel, Ngugi has a tragic scheme of more than adequate scope."[7]

The novel does present a grand scope in time and space. It traces a continuum that goes as far back as Gikuyu and Mumbi, the ancestral founders of Agikuyu. In space, the novel evokes remote lands beyond Kenya and East Africa—Germany, Egypt, Jerusalem, Burma—where characters such as Boro had gone, fighting somebody else's wars, and who now dream of carrying their experiences into a meaningful action, an odyssey toward regaining their own freedom. So, in a sense, *Weep Not, Child* is a microcosm, indeed a narrative matrix of the larger epic narrative that is subsequently continued in Ngugi's other novels. If it is "a novel of childhood,"[8] then it celebrates the birth of a generation of freedom fighters resolutely bent on transforming Mugo wa Kibiro's prophecies into reality in order to establish a bridge between their present and past on the one hand and to sow the grain of wheat that appears to germinate in *Petals of Blood* on the other. It is, indeed, the overwhelming restlessness of such a spirit—i.e., social force—that conveys a sense of tragic imprisonment in the small confines of Ngugi's first published novel. This restless spirit is later on released in *A Grain of Wheat* and *Petals of Blood*, where it finds a fuller, more detailed expression.

In addition to the grand span in time and space, *Weep Not, Child* gives a prominent place to myth, prophecy, and land. Here the narrator evokes the beginnings of the so-called Mau Mau uprising and outlines the parameters—both human and natural—within which it takes place. We shall show how it progressively builds up on a select number of episodes cast in mythic language; how it stresses, on every occasion—especially in myths and prophecies—the importance of the land issue; and finally, how this microcosm paves the way for *A Grain of Wheat*, which of necessity leads to *Petals of Blood*.

Creation Myth

Weep Not, Child opens with a description of the town of Kipanga, characterized by dual oppositions between village (Mahua) and town (Kipanga); road and track; valleys and plains; the rough and sickly land of the black people and the green land of the white people. At the end of this descriptive passage, the image of "four ridges that stood and watched one another" brings the entire scene into focus.

Yet, it is in Kipanga that the narrator's attention is drawn to the peculiar image of a man presented as the prophet-god of the Indian people. From the Indian shops of Kipanga, the towering shadow of Mahatma Gandhi looms into the narrative as the celebrated leader of the Indians; a messiah whom they venerate and respect. In the African community, it is even rumored that Gandhi is the god of the Indians. The image of Mahatma Gandhi and the struggle of the Indians for freedom appear exemplary to the Gikuyu in their quest for freedom.

> There was a man in India called Gandhi. This man was a strange prophet. He always dressed poorly in calico stretched over his body. Walking along the shops, you could see his photograph in every Indian building. The Indians called him Babu, and it was said this Babu was actually their god. He had told them not to go to war so that while black people had been conscripted into the army the Indians had utterly refused and had been left alone. It was rumored that the White men in Kenya did not like them because they had refused to go to war against Hitler. (*Weep Not*, p. 25)

The presentation of Gandhi establishes a thematic precedent. In the midst of a colony emerges a local messiah who leads his people to freedom, which lends weight to the coming of the Gikuyu leader so often prophesied by the seer Mugo wa Kibiro. The coming of this leader is an essential theme in the novel because of the message of hope and freedom that it carries. It is especially important to the African peasants who have lost their land to the white settlers, but they see the coming of the messiah as a precondition of the recovery of their land. Their claim to the land goes as far back as their ancestors Gikuyu and Mumbi. Ngotho's faith in the prophecy is sustained by his underlying belief in the divine power of Murungu, creator of the ancestors.

Ngotho's belief in Murungu handing over the land of the ridges to the Gikuyu is revealed when, in a familial scene, Nyokabi induces him to tell their children a story. As it turns out, the story is more than a simple folk tale; it is the Gikuyu myth of origin. This is a unique passage in Ngugi's writing for it is the only one in which we find a full account of this myth.

The narrative movement covers four significant stages. The description of the first stage is underscored by violence stemming from natural forces in a world devoid of human life. In this stage, natural phenomena occur and assert their presence: in the beginning "there was wind and rain," as well as thunder and lightning. The second stage reaches its peak with the emergence of the sun, forecasted by the growth of the tree of life that is associated with Gikuyu and Mumbi. The third stage focuses on human activity and movement, from the mountain to the ridges, through Mukuruwe wa Gathanga. This movement of Gikuyu and Mumbi is instigated by the creator, who, like the parents who teach their children to walk by guiding their first steps, takes them to places. In the text, Murungu is obviously the real acting force ("Murungu took Gikuyu and Mumbi from this Holy Mountain . . . He took them to the country of the ridges . . . stood them . . . He finally took them to Mukuruwe wa Gathanga"). In the fourth and last stage, the creator gives the land to Gikuyu and Mumbi with specific instructions for its use.

> There was wind and rain. And there was also thunder and terrible lightning. The earth and the forest around Kerinyaga shook. The animals of the forest whom the Creator had recently put there were afraid. There was no sunlight. This went on for many days so that the whole land was in darkness. Because the animals could not move, they just sat and moaned with wind. The plants and trees remained dumb. It was, our elders tell us, all dead except for the thunder, a violence that seemed to strangle life. It was this dark night whose depth you could not measure, not you or I can conceive of its solid blackness, which would not let the sun pierce through it.
>
> But in this darkness, at the foot of Kerinyaga, a tree rose. At first it was a small tree and grew up, finding a way even through the darkness. It wanted to reach the light, and the sun. This tree had life. It went up, up, sending forth the rich warmth of blossoming tree—you know, a holy tree in the dark night of thunder moaning. This was Mukuyu, God's tree. Now you know that at the beginning there was only one man (Gikuyu) and one woman (Mumbi). It was under this Mukuyu that he first put them. And immediately the sun rose, and the dark night melted away. The sun shone with a warmth that gave life and activity to all things. The wind and lightning and thunder stopped. The animals stopped wondering and moved. They no longer moaned but gave homage to the Creator, and Gikuyu and Mumbi. And the creator, who is also called Murungu, took Gikuyu and Mumbi from His holy mountain. He took them to the country of ridges near Siriana and there stood them on a big ridge before He finally took them to Mukuruwe wa Gathanga about which you have heard so much. But he had shown them all the land—yes, children God showed Gikuyu and Mumbi all the land and told them:
>
> "This land I hand over to you. O man and woman. It's yours to *rule* and *till* in serenity sacrificing only to me, *your god*, under my sacred tree." (*Weep Not*, p. 27; my emphasis)

In the beginning, there was violence. Out of the violence of nature grew the tree of life. Despite the violence and lack of nourishing light, the tree was able to grow up. It is under this tree of life that the Creator placed Gikuyu and Mumbi and, above all, gave them the land. Here lies Ngotho's faith in the inevitable coming of the prophet-leader and, out of chaos, the re-establishment of order. Ngotho reads the myth as a parable of the present, and the prophecy of Mugo wa Kibiro only serves to deepen his faith, to anchor it, as it were, to the fundamental element, the land. The deepening is created by repetition, and repetition serves memory; it emphasizes the presence of things.

The story might have ended as another account of Gikuyu origin myth if Nyorogue, in his innocence, had not asked the question that caused his father to connect the remote past to the present, "Where did the land go?"

(*Weep Not*, p. 47). Ngotho, then, continues his chronicle of the history, recounting the long spell of drought, and the coming of the white man and his subsequent appropriation of the land.

This myth is a myth of origin extended into the chronicle of the history of the peoples of Kenya. It is possible to trace the development and use of Gikuyu myths and legends in Ngugi's writings. It should be noted that if the various narratives echo one another, they do not simply duplicate each other, but expand coherently into a unified body that expresses a situation and registers its evolutions and transformation.

In *The River Between,* the narrator makes reference to Gikuyu and Mumbi in order to remind the antagonistic clans of their common ancestry beyond their individual claims to "spiritual superiority and leadership." Also, he emphasizes their collective right to the land by quoting Murungu: "It [the land] is yours to rule and till, *you and your posterity*" (my emphasis).[9] But in *Weep Not, Child*, the quotation is modified to insist on the necessity of Gikuyu unity in the face of their dispossession:

> This land I hand over to you. O man and woman. It's yours to rule and till in serenity sacrificing only to me, *your god, under my sacred tree.* (*Weep Not*, p. 27; my emphasis)

The words "your god" are placed in relief in the sentence. Gikuyu god—not an alien god—should be the center of Agikuyu life. In the context of the Emergency, this is a paramount preoccupation for the landless Ngothos; for how do you sacrifice to Murungu under his "sacred tree" if the very land on which it stands is inaccessible? The modification in the reported spoken words of Murungu registers a modification of directives also: go after the land, it seems to say. It is precisely in such instances that *Weep Not, Child* differs clearly from *The River Between*, while it indicates a new turn in Ngugi's writing, from the dramatization of a cultural antagonism to an open political conflict, with land as the issue instead of circumcision.

The Land

The land issue is at the heart of *Weep Not, Child*. The loss of the land is tragic and its recovery vital for the African peasants. The knowledge of this situation only heightens Ngotho's sorrows, but it is not only his consciousness of the trap of history that makes his predicament so painful. The quality of the hurt that he experiences is intensified by the fact that he ends up working on the very land that had been stolen from him in order to guarantee the welfare of the imposter. On a daily basis, Ngotho is confronted with the painful reminder of his plight and the image of his failure as the custodian of the sacred land-temple trusted upon him by his ancestors.

The love that Mr. Howlands nurtures for the same piece of land has often been compared to Ngotho's attachment to the land. Aside from the dubious origin of his ownership of the property (Mr. Howlands can justifiably be read as Mr. *How lands*), Howlands's attachment to the land has a different quality: it is of a very recent origin and, as such, cannot claim the support of tradition. Ngotho's relation to the land, on the other hand, goes as far back as the creation of the first human beings; it is an absolute truth that sustains his hope in a better future. Whereas Howlands relies on a strong individual ownership of the land, Ngotho sees the land as ancestral communal property. For him the land is not only a source of livelihood, but life itself.[10] In the words of the narrator, "Ngotho was too much a part of the farm to be separated from it" (*Weep Not*, p. 53). Of course, in the case of a peasant economy, removing the land from the peasant amounts to cutting off his life support system; hence the impossibility of a reconciliation between the settler colonialist and the dispossessed African peasant is, at this point, sealed off.

This tension around the land issue becomes apparent early in the novel when Njoroge asks Ngotho, "Where did the land go?" (*Weep Not*, p. 47). Ngotho is compelled to give his audience a coherent explanation of the way in which successive events led to the landlessness of Africans. It appears that the British settlers have gradually succeeded in appropriating the land from Africans who had been weakened by a long spell of drought of uncertain origin.

The Prophecy

There is a close relation between Ngotho's unflinching faith in his right to the land and the strong hope that, despite his sad condition, he has to recover the lost land. This relation is built on, and sustained by, the prophecies of Mugo wa Kibiro, the celebrated Gikuyu seer who is often referred to in Ngugi's novels. The reader of Ngugi's novels has been acquainted with him in *The River Between*, when he said to his people,

> Arise—Heed the prophecy. Go to the mission place—Learn all the wisdom and all the secrets of the white man. But do not follow his vices. Be true to your people and the ancient rites.[11]

The man who foretold the arrival of the white man and the building of the railway has also predicted the coming of the black messiah, a leader whose arrival will bring about the restitution of the land of the Gikuyu. If, in spite of every obstacle, Ngotho keeps a strong faith in Mugo's prophecy, it is because all the preceding ones had been painfully true.

Prophecies, we have observed, are also a structural device for the epic story; they allow the action of the story to unfold smoothly. The teleological movement that guides Ngotho stems from a line of unfailing prophecies and his strong faith in the eventual fulfillment of the present prophecy. In a sense, this prophecy is already in the myth of origin of the Gikuyu; Mugo's prophecies are no more than a reaffirmation of the established semantic development we find in the myth of origin. We know the beginning, and we are aware of the end. Whatever happens in between is a part of the necessary ordeal that leads to the fulfillment of the prophecy, the self-realization of the spirit of Murungu.

In *The River Between*, this prophecy is interpreted by Chege as a myth of education. School education in the ways and secrets of the white man was expected to bring freedom, and when the white people denied the Gikuyu the use of their schools, the Gikuyu built separate schools. The people believe in the words of the seer when he says, "Go to the mission place—Learn all the wisdom and all the secrets of the white man." The theme of education continues to occupy a place in *Weep Not, Child* in Njoroge's obsession with education; nevertheless, it is treated as a less serious issue, as a piece of the adorning artifacts of a child's romantic vision of the world.

Mugo's prophecy relative to the arrival of a black messiah is what keeps Ngotho alive, hopefully waiting. It not only makes him a believer in the inexorability of freedom and in the recovery of the lost land, it also turns Ngotho into a passive man. The frequency with which the word "waiting" is applied to him in the text is simply overpowering. Ngotho seems to surrender to his present condition with the belief that it will end someday. How do we explain Ngotho's attitude? Is it caused by impotent old age faced with seemingly unsurmountable events? Or does it develop from the deeply mystical thought of a man who lives in a world that is completely fraught with mystical beliefs? Whatever explanation we choose needs to be placed in the context of colonialism. Ngotho is a product of colonialism as much as Boro is a by-product of it. In the words of Fanon, "The first thing which the native (the colonized person) learns is *to stay in his place*, and not go beyond certain limits."[12]

In contrast to his father, Boro does not approve of passivity. He does not believe in prophecies—not even in Mugo's promised leader-savior. He despises his father's inactive attitude in the face of tyranny. If his father is a victim, then Ngotho shows no compassion for him. In contrast to his father, Boro is a man of action. He advocates violence as a means to recover their lost land and, with it, their dignity. He quickly dismisses the prophecy as an irrelevant superstition and wonders how could these people have let the white man occupy the land without acting and, worse still, how can they continue serving the man who has taken their land?

The opposition between father and son is polarized in the father's reluctant passivity and the son's determination for active resistance. When the land returns to the people, it will be brought by violent action—everything else having failed—informed by hope, some measure of optimism in victory. Ironically Boro, who does not believe in prophecies, is one of those who, as freedom fighters, helped Kenya gain self-government.

As for Ngotho, he waits and dies, like his father, who having lost his land, "Died lonely, a poor man *waiting* for the white man to go" (*Weep Not*, p. 48). While "*waiting* for the prophecy to be fulfilled," Ngotho hires himself out to work on the very piece of land that his father once owned.

He is conscious of the anathema that this waiting surrounds him with and humiliates him in the eyes of his own children. On the morning following his conversation with the children, Ngotho remembers how

> The voice of Boro had cut deep into him, cut into all the lonely years of *waiting*. Perhaps he and others had *waited* for too long and now he feared that this was being taken as an excuse for inactivity or, worse, a betrayal. (*Weep Not*, p. 52; my emphasis)

Weep Not, Child ends in the destruction of Ngotho's family by the violence of the Emergency. The introduction of the State of Emergency announces the general mood that prevails in *A Grain of Wheat*, where violence appears in its psychological, ideological, and physical forms. Moreover, it is in *A Grain of Wheat* that Boro's advocacy and use of violence is revived by Kihika in the scene of his meeting with Mugo in particular (*Grain*, pp. 215-19).

The Messiah

Although Boro declares his contempt for what he calls "superstitious beliefs" in a future messiah, there is no doubt that during the Emergency he became one of the people who surrounded Jomo Kenyatta as their leader and who responded to his call for a general uprising against the colonial government. As a freedom fighter, Boro participated in the armed struggle and partook of the creation of the Jomo symbolism in its most durable form: the embodiment of freedom. Indeed the freedom fighters are the people who backed the prophecy of Mugo wa Kibiro and gave it some substance, body, and soul by bringing it to fruition.

Jomo is often referred to as the much-awaited messianic leader in Ngugi's novels. In *Weep Not, Child*, the narrator says,

> There was a man sent from God whose name was Jomo. He was the Black Moses empowered by God to tell the white Pharaoh "Let my people go." (*Weep Not*, p. 88)

As he likened the Gikuyu people with "the children of Israel," Njoroge came to the conclusion that

> although all men were brothers, the black people had a special mission to the world because they were the chosen people of God. This explained his brother's remark that Jomo was the Black Moses. (*Weep Not*, p. 78)

The same idea is repeated throughout *A Grain of Wheat*. On the day of Uhuru celebration,

> They [the people] sang of Jomo (he came, like a fiery spear among us), his stay in England (Moses sojourned in the land of Pharaoh) and his return (he came riding on a cloud of fire and smoke) to save his children. He was arrested, sent to Lodwar, and on the third day came home from Maralal. He came riding on a chariot home. The gates of hell could not withhold him. Now angels trembled before him. (*Grain*, p. 15)

The reader is reminded of a similar passage devoted to Mahatma Gandhi. Repetition is a characteristic of symbolism. The image of a leader engraved in the prophecies of Mugo is offered again and again in various figures throughout the narrative.

Beti also uses symbolic recurrences in his novels. As the narrative proceeds, the *Creator* disappears, leaving the stage for the old wise man of Ekoundoum who, as a prophet, plays the important role of mediator; after him, Mor-Zamba occupies the center of the narrative, alternating with Ruben and Ouragan-Viet. Of the three characters, Ruben is like Jomo in Ngugi's novels—the closest to an embodiment of a second mediator. Nowhere to be seen, he nevertheless occupies an important part in the narrative; his words and actions, which are all related to the efforts of his organization and people, permeate all things and influence the course of the entire narrative; his invisibility is equal to the invisibility of Jomo among the familiar characters in the novels.

In Ngugi's works, Jomo is portrayed as the leader, and although the same semantic reading is applied to both characters, Jomo is given a bigger representation than Gandhi. Ngugi uses two narrative models that inform the entire story of *Weep Not, Child*. These narrative models are the legend of Gandhi and the Gikuyu creation myth. As the presentation of Gandhi paves the way for the emergence of the Gikuyu leader-savior, so does the creation myth prepare the terrain for the atmosphere of violence that characterizes the novel. The parallel between Gandhi and Jomo is obvious enough, but the violence is merely suggested in the creation myth in the birth pangs of human life neatly associated with nature (cf. the tree of life). There is, lying dormant in this single narrative, Ngugi's obsessive theme of the quest for life; the necessity for the grain to die before its eventual rebirth into something greater; the quest for the lost land and for freedom. The operative methods of the search are sometimes explored in school education, as the people seek out the "secrets" of the white man, or in armed struggle, as it turns out in *A Grain of Wheat*. In a general fashion, this question is simply a quest for light in an obscure labyrinth, but to be more specific, it is a quest for a transformational knowledge. Society, no longer at ease, is feverishly seeking, against the forces of disaster, a greater, more adequate, form of living.

Both Ngugi and Beti share in this vision, which is suggested in *Weep Not, Child* and *Remember Ruben*. Otherwise, how do we account for the tribulations of Mor-Zamba, and especially, for the long quest of Abena for a gun in Europe and Asia, far beyond the corners of his native land? The immediate cause is social, as Mor-Zamba loses a young bride to an old man who enjoys the support of the tyrannical faction of elders led by Engamba. This event highlights a time of darkness for the traditional democratic institutions grimly illustrated by the coup d'état of Engamba's party. Abena decides that there is fault with the way things are run. His analysis of the situation leads him to the conclusion that the oppressed man needs to invest less in his search of a wife and more in his quest for a gun. Obviously, these two terms (wife and gun), which are graphically polarized in the novel, have a symbolic import.

In *Weep Not, Child*, the reader discovers a cobweb of myths and legends that not only dramatizes the past of the Gikuyu, but also serves as the form that carries a certain vision of history. (I have suggested that Ngotho's teleological view of historical developments is guided by his faith in the prophecy of Mugo wa Kibiro.) This vision of history leans on the collective understanding of events (use of popular myths and legends) and explains the individual by the collective in a cosmological order.[13]

The quest for freedom that takes Abena and Mor-Zamba far away from their native home is pursued and unraveled in a sequel. Although Ngugi does not present his narrative as a sequel in terms of identifying the same characters in subsequent books, the quest for freedom that is outlined in *Weep Not, Child* remains central to the novels that follow it. It is a long quest that goes even beyond the advent of self-rule into a new era when life has already assumed, in many ways, a new form and when oppression, being internally inflicted, must be combatted with new means. The next chapter will examine the symbolic significance of these odysseys.

Notes 2

[1] Durand, Gilbert, *Les Structures anthropologiques de l'imaginaire* (Paris: Bordas, 1969).

[2] For a study of the theme of orphanhood, see Joseph Awouna, "Le conte africain et la société traditionnelle," *Présence Africaine*, no 66 (1968): 137-44, and Gerald Storzer, "Abstraction and Orphanhood in the Novels of Mongo Beti," *Présence Francophone*, no. 15 (1977): 93-112.

[3] Isidore Okpewho, *The Epic in Africa* (New York: Columbia University Press, 1979), 86.

[4] Ibid., 85.

[5] Ibid., 86.

[6] Djibril Tamsir Niane, *Sundiata: An Epic of Old Mali* (London: Longman, 1965); Charles Bird with Mamadou Koita and Bourama Soumaoro, *The Songs of Seydou Camara, Volume One: Kambili*, Occasional paper in Mande Studies (Bloomington: African Studies Center, Indiana University, 1974); and Daniel Biebuyck and Kahombo C. Mateene, eds., *The Mwindo Epic from the Banyanga (Congo Republic).* (Berkeley and Los Angeles: University of California Press, 1969).

[7] Gerald Moore, *Twelve African Writers* (Bloomington: Indiana University Press 1980), 270.

[8] Ibid., 269.

[9] Ngugi wa Thiong'o [James Ngugi], *The River Between* (London: Heinemann, 1974), 2.

[10] See Jomo Kenyatta, *Facing Mount Kenya* (London: Martin Secker & Warburg Ltd., 1938; reprint, New York: Random House, 1961), 22.

[11] Ngugi, *River*, 24.

[12] Frantz Fanon, *The Wretched of the Earth* (New York: Grove Press, 1968), 52.

[13] James Olney, *Tell Me Africa: An Approach to African Literature* (Princeton, N. J.: Princeton University Press, 1974), 122: "By joining legend and autobiography ... the Gikuyu transform their life into a myth. This way of seeing life in mythic terms, whereby every man or at least every Gikuyu—is living out his proper role in an unfolding universal drama whose ultimate author is Yahweh or Ngai, gives a weight and meaning to individual life by placing it within the patterns of ritual history and invests that individual life with a much greater than individual responsibility and significance."

3

The Odyssey
Social Transformations in the Ruben Trilogy

Introduction

The trilogy by Mongo Beti is composed of a tripartite movement: (1) the identification and revolt of the subject, (2) the negative metamorphosis of the subject, and (3) the positive transformation and exaltation of the subject. A novel corresponds to each movement. The movements convey an ongoing social transformation process that takes place in this long narrative.

The first movement of the trilogy is expressed in *Remember Ruben.* In this novel, the writer describes the growth of Mor-Zamba. Two controlling issues run throughout the book. On the one hand, the narrative is the story of the life and adventures of Mor-Zamba. On the other is his relation with Abena; at this level, the narrative appears as the story of a friendship. They both leave Ekoundoum, and while Mor-Zamba is sent to a forced labor camp, Abena enlists in the army, hoping to acquire a gun there. His return fulfills two functions. He intensifies and revitalizes the struggle of the Rubenists for self-rule; he also reveals to Mor-Zamba his real identity. Symbolically, Abena "frees" Mor-Zamba from the prison of ignorance and alienation from the history of his people. This, then, appears to be the immediate function of their friendship.

Characteristically, Mor-Zamba and Abena form a pair, as is often the case in heroic narratives.[1] Also, the tribulations of Mor-Zamba follow the pattern of the heroic songs of *Sundiata, Da Monzon,* or *Moneblum,* where the theme of the initiatory journey of the hero is an essential feature of the narrative.

When considered as the preliminary stage in the composition of the trilogy, *Remember Ruben* appears to depict the context in which the subject of the narrative—i.e., the heroic struggle of the people of Akomo, whose best spirit is exemplified in Ruben, Abena, and Mor-Zamba—is identified and in which it rebels against its social condition.

This preliminary stage is crucial because it allows the novelist to lay the mythological foundation, Akomo, on which he builds the subsequent social transformations. This stage identifies the origin of the rebellion and indicates the ways and means of ending social alienation. As the alienation of Mor-Zamba is symbolic of the alienation of his people, his recovery of his true identity suggests the potential recovery of their identity by his fellow countrymen. But this general recovery is far from materializing yet in the narrative. As the old saying goes, "Even in the darkest of the night, one may journey all the way to Timbuctu." Mor-Zamba may journey toward this liberation, but he knows nothing of the obstacles that lie ahead. Nonetheless, the closure of *Remember Ruben* is satisfactory because it occurs only after providing an answer to the question of identification raised at the beginning of the novel; at the end of the novel, the reader learns the true identity of Mor-Zamba, the foundling.

As in Ngugi's *A Grain of Wheat*, there is the myth of the black messiah in *Remember Ruben*. In the city and in the country, workers and peasants firmly believe that someday there will come a black messiah to lead them out of "Sodome and Gomorrah." They see this messiah in Ruben; herein lies their reluctance to believe that he has been killed when the government announces his death.

The narrator calls the world of *Perpetua* "Sodome and Gomorrah." The novel represents the second stage of the trilogy and the negative transformation of *Remember Ruben*. It is characterized by a movement downward as a symbolic descent in hell. The preceding novel's subject, the heroic struggle of the people of Akomo, is now reduced to a voice of hopelessness. Like Oedipus, and Bakary Dian of the epic of *Da Monzon*, it is struck by tragic blindness. *Perpetua* continues the odyssey of the struggle, and it represents the obstacles that lay ahead on the journey to "Timbuctu." In the journey of the subject, *Perpetua* represents the moment of ritual cleansing.

With the exception of Ekoundoum and Zombotown, a new shantytown, *Perpetua* and *Remember Ruben* share the same setting. The link between the two novels is more strongly indicated by the narrator's numerous references to events that happened during the era depicted in *Remember Ruben*. In an effort to explain current events, the narrator evokes events described in *Remember Ruben*. Also, the historic link between the two eras is highlighted through the protagonist investigator. He is a former militant of the P. P. P., the Rubenist party that emerged in *Remember Ruben*. The decade that separates the end of *Remember Ruben* from *Perpetua* is one of negative transformations. The narrative unfolds as the enterprise of reconstruction of the deconstructed life of Perpetua; it reveals a transformation of the subject from a colonial, yet hopeful, situation to neocolonialism and near-absolute hopelessness. The changes are registered through the contrastive perspective of Essola. The negative metamorphosis of the subject appears in three modes: the deconstructed vision of the life of Perpetua, the dislocation of family ties, and the degradation of society at large.

At another level, *Perpetua* attempts to demystify "independence" and the French concept of "decolonization" as it was applied to African countries. *Perpetua* is also a ritual depiction of the mythical Africa of social instability and immemorial hardships. The novel stresses this tragic myth of perpetual failure even as it demystifies "decolonization."

Lament (subtitled *Remember Ruben 2* in the original version) represents the positive radical transformation of the subject. Here, the reader witnesses a process of total transformation; the subject is revitalized and exalted in the narrative. "Timbuctu" is in sight, perhaps at hand, when the novel closes. *Lament* represents the celebration of life in a movement upward, elevating society to a loftier stage. It presents individual, collective, and institutional transformations.

Beti relies on historical cases of guerilla warfare—unnamed though they are in this particular segment of the odyssey—as a support system for the myth of liberation that he creates. The novel is a microcosm of methods of guerrilla warfare. Typically, the freedom fighters leave the city to fight in the rural areas. They use a "hit and run" strategy and seek to capture weapons from the enemy. They rely on the peasants for food and shelter, and encourage them to rebel against their oppressor. The guerrillas retreat inside a neighboring country when necessary. They form the people's army, which is underfed, underclothed, and underarmed, yet they strike and win small victories. When they establish a "liberated zone" (e.g., the infirmary), they use it as a stepping stone in the struggle over a "contested zone" (the palace of the despot chief and the mission). Theirs is a rugged, unconventional army, where the absence of badges on a uniform does not preclude official titles. Thus, Mor-Zamba is called General; Mor-Kinda, Commander; and Evariste is promoted to the rank of lieutenant.

Remember Ruben

Structural Organization and Plot Development

A Quest for Identity

Remember Ruben is divided into two parts, each bearing a thematically significant title. Part one, composed of six chapters, is titled "Everything for a Wife, Nothing for a Gun." Part two, composed of eight chapters, centers on the odyssey of Abena and Mor-Zamba; it is appropriately called "Fugitive and Tormented."

In terms of textual organization, the novel appears on the surface as the narrative of the life of Mor-Zamba, describing the growth of a foundling from a shy, but sensitive, child to a naive, yet strong and generous, teenager who becomes a responsible adult and leader of freedom fighters. As such, it displays a symmetrical structure on the spatio-temporal level. Part one describes the life of Mor-Zamba from Ekoundoum, where he first appears, to Oyolo. Part two covers the years between World War II and the advent of self-rule in 1960. Thus, each part of the novel covers a period of roughly fifteen years. At the conclusion of the novel, when Abena instructs Mor-Zamba to return to Ekoundoum to liberate the city from the dictatorship of the local chief, Mor-Zamba is a young man in his mid-thirties. The end of the novel suggests the projection of a reverse symmetry.

Although one could follow several other approaches for a study of the development of *Remember Ruben,* there is room for an analysis of the novel as a linear account of the life of Mor-Zamba.[2] However, the narrative advances through a rhythmic movement characterized by waves of hope and hopelessness. This is a contrastive narrative technique whereby plot development is carried through the depiction of alternating periods of tension and relaxation.

The first person the orphaned Mor-Zamba meets at the city gates is Engamba, who immediately attacks the child and remains hostile to him during his stay in Ekoundoum. Luckily the old man welcomes him and adopts him. A series of attacks are perpetrated against Mor-Zamba, while the old man desperately tries to protect him. There is a sign of relief as Mor-Zamba becomes a friend of Abena and finds acceptance among the citizens of Ekoundoum. These hopeful signals are destroyed again by Engamba and his party when the old man tries to help his adopted son get married. A series of disputes and tensions emerges. Mor-Zamba is framed. He is detained and subjected to forced labor at Camp Gouverneur Leclerc. When he gets out of detention, he stumbles into the slums of Oyolo. Toussaint-Louverture, the African district on the outskirts of the opulent colonial city of Oyolo, is a shantytown infested with rats, disease, and hunger. It is a haven for the poor, the depressed, and the wretched.

> Toussaint-Louverture, the principal African quarter of Oyolo, had only received this name, in a spirit of derision, with the arrival of the first wounded black survivors from the desert battles, mainly Kufra and Bir-Hakeim. The colonial administration suspected them of exerting a certain moral influence on their compatriots by repeating distorted and embittered tales about their life alongside the white troops, often with deliberate exaggeration, and so saw in them the revolutionary mob of some future black terror.
> (*Ruben*, p. 81)

The stay in Toussaint-Louverture benefits Mor-Zamba in two ways. He receives a letter from Abena, who plans to come back with a gun to free the people from the shackles of colonialism. Also, Mor-Zamba hears of Ruben, a god-like black messiah who brings hope to the poor people of the slums. This leader of the African workers' union appeared three times during the two years Mor-Zamba spent in Toussaint-Louverture (*Ruben*, p. 84).

At the same place, Mor-Zamba witnesses the violence of colonial rule as the police fire into a crowd of protesting youngsters, killing a hundred of them. Slowly, the episode of Ekoundoum, the detention camp, and the violence in Toussaint-Louverture coalesce to give the foundling his first sense of political awareness.

The contrastive narrative mode that emerges in part one of *Remember Ruben* continues in part two within a larger framework of events. Thus, there is tension in the air when Mor-Kinda announces that Ruben is a prisoner of the colonial authorities. The hope hitherto entertained by the Rubenists begins to fall apart. Fortunately, Mor-Zamba frees Ruben. But no sooner does this happen than the colonial forces intensify the repression on a mass scale in order to track down all suspected Ruben sympathizers. Along with the increased repression, the people of Kola-Kola helplessly witness the rise to power of Baba Toura, the sworn enemy of Ruben. Ruben "loses" the farcical elections to the colonial stooge. With a measure of hope, the militants learn of the imminent return of Abena, but they also learn of the official ban imposed on Ruben's party. For Mor-Zamba and the Rubenists, despair once again replaces hope. The people of Kola-Kola discover that, despite his usual cautiousness, the man who embodied their dream of salvation has fallen in the course of the struggle. The days are indeed bleak for the slum-dwellers.

> Most people in Kola-Kola think that now Ruben's dead the authorities believe they have elbow-room to dole us out an independence in their own style: first of all, they want to place at the head of affairs a man of their own, a politician whose blackness extends only to his skin. That's already done, really—its Baba Toura the Biture; with him in office, one step is already taken. As he is invincibly docile, they want to use him as the perfect screen; behind him, they will continue to govern and everything will go on as before. We will have independence, but nothing will be changed. (*Ruben*, p. 217)

The narrative reaches a particularly intense level of despair. It is precisely at this point that Hurricane-Viet, hitherto known as Abena, emerges. His return home is reminiscent of the arrival of Akomo in Ekoundoum; he comes with fire. The story ends in a blaze and thus transcends the rhythmic tension and relaxation pattern of the novel. Just when Baba Toura and the colonialists think they are victorious, an unsuspected force delivers a telling blow. Martin T. Bestman, who analyzes the novel as the linear account of the life of Mor-Zamba, concludes that "the last pages of the novel are full of action and promise."[3] They reveal the origin of the wandering child when Abena discloses to Mor-Zamba that he is the direct grandson of the late chief of Ekoundoum, that his grandfather died in "mysterious conditions," that Engamba was irresponsible as a guardian of Mor-Zamba's mother, and that Mor-Zamba could not have married Engamba's daughter anyway, since they were blood relations. The entire narrative is justified by the mystery of the origins of Mor-Zamba, with which the novel opens. It is a quest for identity that is partially satisfied at the end of the novel.

The Life and Adventures of Mor-Zamba

A linear reading of *Remember Ruben* inevitably leads to focus on Mor-Zamba exclusively. The novel becomes the story of his life and adventures. Is such a limiting, exclusive approach permissible? What, if anything, could justify such a perspective?

The first answer to this question lies with the collective narrator's perspective. While recognizing that almost the entire community of Ekoundoum is guilty of various crimes against the orphan child, the narrator is also engaged in an act of ritual purification of his fellow citizens. At the end of *Remember Ruben,* the reader learns that Mor-Zamba is the rightful inheritor of the chiefdom of Ekoundoum; in *Lament,* it becomes obvious that he is the major benefactor of the community that he has freed from the old chief's tyranny. The story is now being told in an effort to restore the truth to the past. In fact, the collective narrator's effort to "confess" the crimes of Ekoundoum reappears in a different form in *Lament*, where Mor-Zamba emerges victorious. Thus, there is a need for the narrator to shed light on the origin and development of the hero of the people of Ekoundoum.

The novel may also appear as the narrative of the transformation of Ekoundoum from a city lost in time and riddled with all sorts of problems, including disease and mistrust under the rule of a despotic chief, to a city where the necessary minimum of justice and equality is guaranteed for every citizen. The narrative, taken from *Lament,* answers the questions How did we get here? and How did the orphan child become the chief of Ekoundoum?

Above all, the narrative of the life of Mor-Zamba allows the reader to "witness" the historic confrontation between the colonial forces and the freedom fighters. The time of the adventures of Mor-Zamba coincides with major political developments in Africa and in the world: World War II and the postwar emergence of nationalist movements for self-rule, including the anticolonial struggles in Indochina and Algeria. All these events affect social life in the country of Mor-Zamba. Also, the odyssey of Mor-Zamba depicts the initiation of a freedom fighter; at this level, the story can be linked with the theme of the initiatory journey as it appears in traditional oral literature.

The Story of a Friendship

In *Remember Ruben*, Mor-Zamba has a companion in Abena. What is the place of Abena in the story? It would be ill-advised to pass over such an important character by limiting our analysis to a focus on Mor-Zamba. The text does not really permit such an exclusive perspective. Abena goes through a great number of obstacles. His odyssey is as important as Mor-Zamba's; in reality, the narrator sees them as a pair and stresses the importance of their brotherhood.[4] Thus, the novel can be seen as the story of their friendship. After all, didn't the two boys adopt each other? Didn't they both go through the experience of injustice and exile from their hometown? Mor-Zamba and Abena are both likened to the ancestral founder of their community. They are seen as heroic, exceptional characters as they build their house; their destinies seem closely linked from then on.

The Ekoundoum episode revolves around the two boys. When Mor-Zamba is detained, Abena leaves the city to look for his friend. A long search reveals the forced labor camp, but he cannot free Mor-Zamba. Abena enlists in the colonial army and serves for twenty-odd years in Europe, Asia, and Africa. There is no direct account of Abena's war experiences, but the reader gets bits and pieces of them from veteran soldiers, such as Maisonneuve and Joseph, who have heard of the gallantries of Abena and returned home. The use of the soldiers' accounts enlarges the narrative perspective while it affords the novel a greater variation of points of view.

Abena returns home at the end of the war, having secured the possession of the gun he sought. His homecoming fulfills a double function. First, he brings hope by leading a fierce urban guerrilla band. Second, he unveils the origin of Mor-Zamba while assigning him a new task.

Though Abena and Mor-Zamba form a pair of friends, they are not twins. The differences that distinguish yet bind them are substantial and many. Some of them appear already in Ekoundoum. Whereas Mor-Zamba exhibits kind understanding, but undue tolerance, for the crimes perpetrated against him by the people of Engamba, Abena remarkably and inexorably turns his back on the corrupt citizens. He seeks to understand their present situation as he engages in a discussion with the old man (*Ruben*, pp. 57-70). Why is a stranger our chief? What happened to our authentic chief? Did we have a chief before the white man imposed one on us? Why did our fathers let the white man impose this chief on us? Rather analytically, Abena pays attention to every event that affects the city of Ekoundoum. He is eager to understand the history of his people. He learns quickly that they live in a society in a state of degeneration. Although Abena leaves the city of his own free will, Mor-Zamba is exiled *manu militari*. Mor-Zamba has a love affair in Ekoundoum, but Abena does not even think of such a thing. Mor-Zamba stays in the country and learns to drive, while Abena leaves as an army driver. Mor-Zamba makes serious mistakes, hesitates sometimes, and shows a lot of naiveté. Abena is always clear on what he intends to achieve and how to go about achieving it. When, finally, the two friends meet again, Mor-Zamba is receiving his first lessons in urban guerrilla warfare, while Abena has become a fierce leader of the freedom fighters.

Remember Ruben is structured on a skillful combination of symmetry and contrast—symmetry but also contrast between characters, time and space, and in the hermeneutics of the plot as well as in its narrative framework. As symmetry underlines resemblances, contrast brings out the contradictory facets of the story. For example, part one is underscored by Mor-Zamba's growing awareness of political and social injustice. The enlightening event is the police massacre of the youth. According to the narrator, it is at this time that Mor-Zamba decides to be more cautious and save himself for the return of Abena.

> Mor-Zamba understood then that he had a mission, to await Abena's return, for which he must keep himself alive and at liberty. (*Ruben*, p. 89)

Likewise, part two of the novel ends on a revelation, with Abena solving the mystery of Mor-Zamba's origin.

The companionship of Mor-Zamba and Abena can be understood in light of the development of social events in Fort-Nègre and Kola-Kola. These events not only shape the future lives of the two men, but they also clarify the nature of their relationship. Abena throws light on the identity of Mor-Zamba and indicates to him a new direction.

> You must go back there. You'll chase away the present chief and become the legitimate one in his place; you'll change everything in Ekoundoum. (*Ruben*, p. 249)

The new task that Abena assigns to Mor-Zamba is not merely to rid the city of Ekoundoum of its despotic chief, but more importantly to restore a sense of pride in the citizens

> in such a way that everyone will be not only happy, which is nothing much, but filled with pride in himself. (*Ruben*, p. 249)

Abena is also a prophet-leader, like Ruben. He is an enlightened leader, a trustworthy guide of his people. There is, lying beneath these characters, the notion of a messianic leadership. Also like Ruben, Abena simply disappears in the night at the end of the novel, becoming even more mysterious as he does not reappear in *Lament*, the sequel to *Remember Ruben*, although his name is evoked everywhere in the second Ekoundoum episode of the trilogy.

Although the differences that bind Mor-Zamba and Abena may be attributed to their contrasting personalities, in terms of political hermeneutics, their relationship becomes that of the avant-garde to the masses, the messianic leader and his freedom fighters. It is the role of the freedom fighters—represented here in Mor-Zamba and Mor-Kinda—to carry the transformation to fruition.[5] Mor-Zamba's quest takes on a more meaningful purpose as he agrees to fulfill his historic responsibility to restore justice and dignity to Ekoundoum. This is the only way to rescue the spirit of Akomo from morbid degeneration.

Time and Space in *Remember Ruben*

From the Time of Akomo to the "Here and Now" of the City
    Remember Ruben is structured around the skillful use of symmetry and contrast. The organization of time fits into the contrastive aspect of the narrative. Eloise A. Brière argues that the country/city dichotomy is coupled with the narrator's use of past and future events to advance the narration.[6] According to Brière, the narrator of *Remember Ruben* uses recollections of events that are posterior or ulterior to the time of the narrated episode in order to reveal more of its significance. This exercise is a combination of flashbacks and projections in the future. Brière discerns eleven flashbacks and eight projections in the future in part one, whereas part two yields only nine flashbacks and twenty projections in the future.
    In part one, past events include the descriptions of the origin of the community, the precolonial life-style, and the subsequent corruption that occurs in the colonial era. Part two favors the projections in the future, but is it simply because Mor-Zamba now lives in the urban environment where the fast rhythm of life hinders the recollection of past events? Although this may appear to be a reasonable assumption, one should not disregard Beti's need to create convincing characters and situations. Since the arrival of Mor-Zamba triggers a chain of reactions and events, it is necessary for the narrator to explain the why and how of these reactions. Some events go far back to the youth of characters, such as Engamba, or to the early days of the community. Since the conflicts in Ekoundoum are also for power, it becomes necessary for the narrator to analyze social structures (or their corruption) that altered the role of the chief. Furthermore, the purpose of the exegesis becomes clearer at the end of the novel, when the origin of Mor-Zamba is revealed.
    The importance of events linked with the present in the narrative of the urban episode has to do with the shift of emphasis imposed on the narrator by the shift in setting. It has been said that the narrator of *Remember Ruben* is a collective narrator who speaks in the communal "we." As all the critics register this aspect, they equally agree that the narrator's confidence in reporting the events of part two, the city episode, dwindles alarmingly. In this part, most pieces of information on the urban life of Mor-Zamba are not the narrator's eyewitness reports. They are obtained from Mor-Zamba himself and from secondary sources that are often difficult to verify.
    The absence of the narrator's eyewitness accounts provides the text with diverse points of view about events. This diversity allows the author to break up the linearity of the narrative, and it provides the audience with a rich and colorful story. It also helps bring to the story a wider scale of experiences, providing a bigger picture of the social situation in the troubled cities. Thus, the projections in the future that are dominant in part two of the story express the contrast between the truly collective "we" of the narrator in part one and the hearsay reports of the events in the city.[7]

The urban episode corresponds with the truly novelistic aspect of this story. The Mor-Zamba portrayed in the city is totally alienated, and the cruelty of the urban setting does not spare him. In the city, uprooted characters, such as father Lobila, have moved away from personal ownership of land in the village to become dispossessed workers. Remnants of their peasant origin are found in father Lobila's dream of going back to the village one day, when he has made enough money to buy land; it is also present in the efforts of his wife to keep a small vegetable garden on the outskirts of the slum area. In addition to the government civil servants and the police force, characters such as Robert, the unsuccessful, but tenacious, businessman, are all a part of the new world of Mor-Zamba; they are urban wage laborers. These people do not necessarily find their sense of community through Akomo, nor do they refer to any creation myths. Their most important myth is freedom. In some instances, they seek to attain it through the accumulation of money: such is the case for father Lobila, Robert, and Jean-Louis, Lobila's teenage son. In this cruel city, the dispossessed find their sense of community in their dream of freedom from their miserable social condition. In this part of the narrative, Mor-Zamba is indeed far removed from the almost pastoral life of Ekoundoum where practically everybody can make a living from the land.

This individualized account of the urban episode is also symptomatic of the alienation that the city-dwellers undergo. If Mor-Zamba has been an outcast in Ekoundoum, he appears more so in the city until he joins the ranks of the Rubenists. It is not surprising that this class of workers is at the forefront of the demand for autonomy and better social conditions.

From the Country to the City

In contrast with the city, Ekoundoum is a much smaller place. It is located between the road and the river, with the forest all around. The activities of its inhabitants seldom go far beyond these limits, except when they cross the river to go to their farms or go into the forest for wood. As for the road, the chief and Van den Rietter, the missionary, are the only ones from Ekoundoum who use it frequently. The world of Ekoundoum seems confined to its ancient limits, cut off from the rest of the country except for a few meetings with its neighbors. Although one senses outside influences gradually creeping in by the road, and through the chief and strangers like Van den Rietter, their presence does not significantly affect the daily life of Ekoundoum before World War II.

The disintegration or corruption of traditional life-style in Ekoundoum is similar to the process Chinua Achebe describes in *Things Fall Apart*. It starts as an internal infection that is aggravated by the arrival of the colonialists and their missionary. If, because it retains aspects of an ancient life-style, Ekoundoum can be painted with the colors of a pastoral setting, there are troubling signs of its imminent downfall. Very quickly in the novel, it appears doomed to lose its quiet and preserved flavor. The isolation and confinement that make the evocation of the pastoral life-style possible are shaky but apparent enough to validate the narrator's "nous." By the end of part one, however, the disruption of the traditional order is all too clear: the soldiers enter Ekoundoum and abduct Mor-Zamba; later on, Abena leaves his native land. These movements in and out of Ekoundoum are done by the road, which comes to represent the medium of the transformation of Ekoundoum. The road is more a symptom than the cause of the infection of the community and its sacred ancestral cult tradition.

The odyssey of Mor-Zamba begins with the detention camp, Camp Gouverneur Leclerc, where he is put to forced labor. It is characterized by confinement and prison brutality. After his release, Mor-Zamba discovers the colonial city of Oyolo and its attendant slum area, Toussaint-Louverture. Oyolo prepares and announces the description of a much bigger city, namely Fort-Nègre, built on the same kind of dichotomy.

The transition from Ekoundoum to the colonial cities is brutal. Camp Gouverneur Leclerc resembles the colonial city in two ways: it is a place where injustice and oppression appear in their militaristic form, and though all the detainees are black, they do not find unity in a common ancestral cult but in their condition as prisoners. It is safe to suggest that Camp Gouverneur Leclerc is a microcosm of the colonial city where everybody is trapped. There is little mention of the movements of people outside the confines of Fort-Nègre/Kola-Kola, aside from the business trips to the country by Robert and Mor-Zamba, and the returning war veterans, Joseph, Maisonneuve, and Hurricane-Viet.

Again contrast and symmetry form the structural nexus of the narrative. The similarity of condition and structure between Oyolo and Fort-Nègre parallels that of Toussaint-Louverture and Kola-Kola. There is, also, a contrast between the colonial district exclusively inhabited by whites and the African slums. This Manichean division—the result of racist colonial policies—has already appeared in Eza Boto's *Ville cruelle*.[8]

Within Fort-Nègre/Kola-Kola itself, the movements are reduced to a single line. In the morning, the slum-dwellers go to work in the colonial district; in the evening, they return to the slums. When the inhabitants of the colonial city go to Kola-Kola, it is often to make an arrest. Nothing but work and repression seem to bind the two districts. The atmosphere is that of an enormous prison where the whites and their black servants (the Saringala police auxiliaries and some civil servants, like Jean-Louis) subject the slum-dwellers to repressive treatment.

Space and time in *Remember Ruben* display a symmetrical evolution. In space, the narrator moves from Ekoundoum to Fort-Nègre, from the countryside to the urban world. In addition to the towns where Mor-Zamba has actually sojourned, the multiplicity of reports from the veterans allows the narrator to evoke distant places in Indochina, Europe, and North Africa. If it lacks the depth of the cosmological dimension of Ekoundoum, part two presents a more detailed picture of the world. In terms of time, it goes from a focus on a fascinating, sometimes mysterious, past to assume the full weight of an obsessive present, ending on a disquieting, yet hopeful, vision of the future. Thus, at the end of *Remember Ruben*, Hurricane-Viet has this vision:

> Africa has been in chains, so to speak, from eternity; whenever we liberate her will be soon enough. Our struggle will be long, very long. Everything you see at this moment in Kola-Kola and throughout the whole colony is nothing but a puerile beginning. Many years from now, or a few months hence, or even after the approaching destruction of Kola-Kola, in the course of which thousands and thousands of our people, women and children among them, will probably die, there will be people to smile at the memory of these preliminary stirrings, as one does in thinking of the innocent games of childhood. Remember Ruben.
> (*Ruben*, p. 252)

Perpetua

Perpetua is the second phase of Beti's trilogy, and it is remarkably different from *Remember Ruben,* though still an integral part of the Ruben cycle. Of all the novels so far written by Beti, none is so pessimistic in outlook, so violent in content, and so overwhelmingly sad in mood. *Perpetua* is a movement downward that is further qualified by the seemingly inexorable invasion of despair. This bottomless pit—the world of *Perpetua*—is the negative transformation of the world of *Remember Ruben*. Its qualitative transformation is made even more obvious by the accumulation of signs of an individual and social degeneration that appear in the novel both historically and psychologically. The fragmented and confused perception of society by the gallery of characters in the novel is the ultimate sign of their loss of balance. *Perpetua* is a tragic novel, and it exemplifies a rather pessimistic tendency in post-independence novels— works such as *The Beautyful Ones Are Not Yet Born*, *Les Soleils des indépendances*, and *Le Cercle des Tropiques* are in the same vein.[9] In these works, the image of what might be expected as a "new society" is sour and repulsive.

In order to show how *Perpetua* is the negative extension of *Remember Ruben,* the following sections will explore the narrative mode, the investigation proper, and the symbolical significance of the novel.

The Narrative Mode in *Perpetua*

The False Linearity of the Narrative

Similar narrative devices are found in both *Perpetua* and *Remember Ruben*. This similarity may be due to the fact that the two novels were written consecutively, if not simultaneously. Their publication in 1974 followed the banning by the French and Camerounian governments of Beti's political essay *Main basse sur le Cameroun.* It broke a decade of literary silence by Beti, suggesting a time of intensive creative writing in order to come back on the literary scene. Significantly, Beti used his long essay as the basis for new fiction.

Perpetua uses contrasts and analogies between the past (depicted in *Remember Ruben*) and the present (as it appears in *Perpetua*), and between cities, individual characters, social attitudes, colonial rule and neocolonial rule, then and now. The analogies may drive readers of *Remember Ruben* to see the past and present as identical, but it soon becomes obvious that the present condition of the country is much worse.

The social picture that emerges out of *Perpetua* is reminiscent of *Remember Ruben* in many ways. Sometimes the present is viewed as a faithful mirror, a duplicate copy, of the past. The tone for this comparative perspective is established as early as the first paragraph of the novel, when the narrator describes the first impressions of Essola, who returns home after six years of imprisonment on 1 December 1961.

> Nothing seemed to have changed except that the long, unbroken covered terraces in front of the ground floor of the shops were now completely deserted. It was as if they had been stripped. (*Perpetua*, p. 1)

The narrator continues, in the following pages, to make references to Ruben and his organization, the days of armed struggle for national liberation, and the social and political climate prevailing then in order to explain the present state of morbid terror in the country.

At another level, *Perpetua* confirms the predictions made in *Remember Ruben.* For example, the reader will recall Mor-Zamba's surprise when he was told that a black president could be as detrimental to his country as the former colonial authority. Baba Toura, the black president in *Perpetua,* is characterized as a bloody dictator.

Constant comparison is the perspective of Essola, the former Rubenist who investigates the death of his sister Perpetua. From this motive, the novel takes on characteristics of police fiction, although only at the level of Essola's activities. But to the narrator of *Perpetua*, this police fiction is only one aspect of the story. The distinction is important because it reveals three levels of apprehension of the novel: the life and death of Perpetua, Essola's investigation of her death, and the investigation of the society by the narrator.

Indeed, *Perpetua* can be read as the story of a woman. In fact, the novel offers hints to that effect; the central story is a story of domestic matters, and everything revolves around Perpetua. More than *Remember Ruben*, *Perpetua* is personalized as the narrative of the miserable life and death of a woman, and the full title of the book appropriately indicates this focus. It is only in that sense that one may speak of a linear account. As the following study of its time structure demonstrates, the narrative as a whole is all but linear.

Time and Space in Perpetua

Essola's investigation is put together so as to offer the entire picture of the situation in which Perpetua died. The reader is presented with the deconstructed elements of her life and death. In order to see a clear chronological order, the reader must reconstruct events. The original text itself, however, bears a complexity that exemplifies the complicated situation that led to the death of Perpetua.

In his excellent study of Beti's novels, Bernard Mouralis[10] shows that there are four essential time periods that make up *Perpetua*:

1. *The colonial period*, which Essola often recalls in order to assess the present, especially in the areas of education and urbanization. The period covers the years from the 1930s through World War II.

2. *Post–World War II period*, with the rise of nationalist demands, the years of guerrilla warfare headed by Ruben and the P.P.P. militants who sought the country's autonomy; the life and death of Perpetua at age twenty in 1967, in the absence of Essola. This period extends into the early years of independence. It is a period of transition for the country.

3. *The duration of Essola's return home*, when part of this time is spent investigating the causes of Perpetua's death. He goes to all the places she lived and talks with the people who knew her, with the exception of her former husband, Edouard, who refuses to see him (July and August 1968).

4. *Essola's investigation*, the final time period, during which the entire investigation as well as the assassination of his brother Martin takes place (August 1968).

The use of these time sequences does not follow a clear chronological order in the novel; it must be reconstructed by the reader. Moreover, the time sequences are distributed unequally in the eight unmarked chapters of the novel. Of the eight chapters only four are directly concerned with the narration of Essola's stay at home: in chapter one, Essola returns home; in chapter two, he travels from Ntermelen to Ngwa Ekeleu, Teuteulen, Oyolo, and Fort-Nègre; in chapter seven, he commits himself to a second trip to Zombotown to inquire about Zeyang, Perpetua's lover; in chapter eight, he assassinates his brother and, again, leaves home. The other chapters (chaps. 3, 4, 5, 6, and parts of 7) describe Essola's efforts to reconstruct his sister's life history from the numerous fragments he gathered from various sources.

If time appears fragmented, the use of space reveals a cobweb of movements in *Perpetua*. There is a constant movement of characters from city to city. This is partly necessitated by the investigation, although Essola himself is a man on the run. Maria, his mother, travels to attend a church ceremony and visit a distant cousin of hers at Ngwa Ekeleu (*Perpetua*, p. 271). Katri also goes to church. Amougou goes to his in-laws'. All these departures allow Essola to be alone with Martin. Even Martin reveals that he had once traveled to Oyolo. Accounts of travels to distant places are abundant in the novel. The unstable, insecure, and nervous vein of the narrative transpires through the high frequency of movements of its characters.

Movement in *Perpetua* is also a function of its chosen narrative mode. The murder inquiry demands that the investigator visits the places where the victim lived; hence, Essola's constant traveling. Essola's movements in turn allow the narrator to visit and investigate the whole country. This becomes the ultimate dimension of the novel. Without the movements of Essola, the reader would have little chance of "seeing" the transformation of the country. Essola's assessment of the transformation is abundantly supplemented by the narrator's comments that are dispersed throughout the story.

The country described in *Remember Ruben* changed dramatically under a black regime. Essola rediscovers his country and tries to assess its condition by comparing it to the past. He realizes that very little has changed in the countryside and in the city, but whenever he registers a transformation, it is for the worse. For example, the youth have deserted the country, leaving the old behind. Terror is present everywhere, and the rural communities give the impression of ghost villages.

> It was as if the whole countryside had been hurriedly abandoned by its population, in terror at the approach of a marauding horde. (*Perpetua*, p. 4)

Also, Essola soon discovers that the country is seriously infected by alcoholism. His own brother suffers from the disease. The new regime, as if to destroy the youth, liberalized the making of a particularly potent local drink (known as "Le bienheureux Joseph" in *Remember Ruben*) called Karkara. In a conversation with the Greek bus driver, he learns other sad things about his country, including the untamed arrogance of the whites toward the blacks. Helplessly, but shamefully, Essola witnesses his own brother's humiliation as the Greek bus driver slaps the drunken man in an effort to get him off the road. Essola denies knowing the poor fellow.

Essola rediscovers Oyolo and Fort-Nègre, the main cities presented in *Remember Ruben*. Cousin Amougou and Essola arrive at Oyolo (*Perpetua*, p. 67), the second phase of the investigation proper. The scenery has not changed very much except for the introduction of Zombotown in the narrative: Zombotown is built on the model of Toussaint-Louverture, but, as the name suggests, it evokes a town of zombies; a kind of ghost town similar to the villages but without any of the beauty and charm of the countryside (*Perpetua*, pp. 44-45).

The Investigation: An Autopsy of the Neocolonial State

The major thread of the narrative in *Perpetua* is the investigation into the death of Essola's sister.   The narrator uses the results of Essola's investigation to shed light on the general condition of the country and to show that the individual history of Perpetua can only be coherently comprehended in its diverse dimensions when placed in a wider social context. As the colonial state is the background of *Remember Ruben*, the neocolonial state is the canvas of *Perpetua*. If it is true that Perpetua's suffering has psychological as well as moral reasons, some aspects of her destiny cannot be isolated from the general social and political conditions that prevail in her country.

The following sections of this book attempt to identify the cause or causes of Perpetua's death; assess the role of Essola in the tragic story and the role of the community at large, in particular, the place occupied by Perpetua's closest relations; and finally, suggest ways in which Perpetua may be perceived in a symbolical dimension that goes beyond a country to represent a larger social system.

The Causes of the Death of Perpetua: Domestic, Psychological, or Political?

Essola's investigation, although rich in testimonies, does not turn up a single eyewitness account of Perpetua's ultimate agony. No one saw her dying. No one was at her deathbed. The only account given is the discovery of the corpse by the teenage houseboy. Anna-Maria, who is practically her adopted mother, runs in to see the pregnant Perpetua stretched on her bed, dead (*Perpetua*, pp. 264-65).

Although the actual circumstances of her death remain unknown, Essola gathers a good sample of information from which he tries to identify the causes of the death. He hopes to prove his mother guilty of the death of Perpetua by selling her away, that is, by requesting from her future son-in-law an unreasonable amount of money as bride-wealth.

> He pieced together in writing all the events and circumstances of Perpetua's death using his sister's school exercise books that Crescentia had given him. In these, sometimes up to half the pages of the book were unused. Capriciously—or perhaps there was some fashion or superstition about it—the little schoolgirl had always stopped using her exercise books before she had filled them up. (*Perpetua*, p. 62)

When he finishes reconstructing the circumstances of his sister's death, does he know yet the real cause of her death (*Perpetua*, p. 91)? Who or what is responsible for the death of Perpetua: her mother, Martin, Edouard, the city authorities, the lack of medical care? Essola is not sure; he slips into a deep lethargy (*Perpetua,* p. 271).

In the course of his investigation, Essola hears many interpretations, reasons, and explanations of the death of Perpetua. In some cases, people see the matter as the result of a domestic conflict or the consequence of immorality. Cousin Amougou believes that nobody should get involved in this family tragedy. For Martin, it is both a matter of family quarrel and an immoral act stemming from his sister's involvement with another man while still married to Edouard. When his sister begs for his help, Martin simply brushes her off with his dubious sense of respect for tradition.

> Well, as I told her, I don't get mixed up in things like that. You don't come into the world to get tangled up in that kind of situation. Our ancestors taught us to steer clear of quarrels between husband and wife. As they say, between tree and bark it's dangerous to poke your finger. (*Perpetua*, p. 207)

Her mother, Maria, being on the defensive, blames fate in the death of Perpetua.

Anna-Maria, Perpetua's adoptive mother and friend, is among those who link the death of Perpetua to some psychological cause. She argues that Perpetua died because she had ceased to care, after enduring a lot of repression. Likewise, Zeyang thinks that she had been so brutalized by Edouard that it was unclear whether she wanted to live any longer (*Perpetua*, p. 55).

As for Antonia, she insists that the absence of a father figure around the girl, more than anything else, caused the death of Perpetua.

> You were the one who was supposed to be father to us, and not only did you never pay any attention to us, but what was worse, when you left college what did you do? Left—just abandoned us. (*Perpetua*, p. 60)

Crescentia and Stephano give political explanations for the death of Perpetua. By describing the efforts of Perpetua to fulfill her dream of becoming a doctor, Crescentia also explains why these efforts failed. The first cause is the obstacles that colonialism creates against the progress of Africans. The second cause of Perpetua's failure is the traditional society that relegates women to a position of second-class citizens. Stephano is more explicitly political in his assessment of the disastrous conditions that prevail in the country. He links Perpetua's death to a lack of medical care, demonstrating that the dictatorship of Baba Toura is guilty of negligence and irresponsibility (*Perpetua*, p. 51).

All these interpretations reflect partial understandings of the plight of Perpetua. It is obvious that nobody has known her from childhood to death; no one saw nor understood everything about her, and each person that came into contact with Perpetua only knew one or two aspects of her personality and her life. Therefore, the interpretations, although often legitimate, are always incomplete.

It is this fragmentary image that Essola sets out to correct for himself— when he left home, his sister was merely a child—and in order to prove his mother guilty of selling her away. He succeeds in doing both by gathering the necessary testimonies to confirm his suspicions. But the mother's role hardly needs proving, and his alcoholic brother's irresponsibility is obvious as soon as Essola arrives home from detention. What purpose, then, does the execution of Martin serve? He was already seriously maimed by alcoholism. Is it a satisfactory response to the victimization of Perpetua? After all, it appears in the narrative, through the testimonies of Crescentia and Amougou, that there are many Perpetuas in the country. It would be more efficient to attack the disease at its very roots. Does the death of Martin, then, serve a personal vendetta for Essola?

The Dilemma of a Freedom Fighter: The Guilty Conscience of Essola

The various explanations offered by the close friends and relations of Perpetua are presented as individually sufficient for an understanding of the cause of her death. Nevertheless, the terrible, perhaps more painful, explanation the investigator hears is that his irresponsibility, his carelessness, his absence from home, caused his sister's destruction. In the eyes of many, including Crescentia and Perpetua's older sister Antonia, Essola is guilty of abandoning his sister to the lurking dangers of the cruel society. If he had stayed home to help his sister instead of joining the freedom fighters, Perpetua, it is believed, would have still been alive. The man who, on hearing of his sister's death, forsook everything political he had until then held on to, is now helpless and practically crushed by the realization of his role in her death. By now, the investigation has gone beyond its initial goal and turned against Essola himself. It is an ironic case of the investigator investigated, so to speak, by his own investigation. In the course of the inquiry, indeed Essola does not just rediscover his country, reconstitute an image of his departed sister, and prove his mother guilty. Quite unexpectedly, he also rediscovers himself, partly in the eyes of others. For example, he recognizes how much war and prison have transformed him into a new person (*Perpetua*, p. 56).

Besides the painful memories of his detention, Essola carries in him the weight of his defection from a dismantled organization that still lives honorably in the memories of the brutalized masses of his country. With the exception of Edouard, everyone else, including Norbert, the chief of police, admires Essola as a kind of hero. But he is tormented by his betrayal of the struggle and dares not reveal the price he paid for his release from detention.

He did not tell his cousin that he had to take out

> a Party card and even agree to act as an organizer for Baba Toura in the area where he was working. These were the conditions of his release and the privilege of a teaching job at the secondary school in Mimbo, a town in the east. (*Perpetua*, p. 20)

Although he agrees to this tyrannical deal only after hearing the disastrous news of his sister's death, he realizes that it is too late to save Perpetua. It is interesting to note, in this regard, the parallel established between Essola and Perpetua, for Perpetua also gave in to the desire of M'Barg'Onana with the hope of finally communicating with her detained brother. Even while they are separated by oppressive conditions, their love and compassion for each other remains strong.

Essola makes a more profound discovery when he realizes that he is a misfit in his rediscovered country. The miserable material conditions of his people, the climate of political terror aggravated by an extended State of Emergency, the prevailing atmosphere of cynicism, and the general fearful and submissive attitude of his people all contribute to create a deep feeling of uneasiness in Essola. Of course, he is unable to explain why everybody seems passive in the face of so much suffering. At the end of his stay, Essola realizes that very little had changed during his absence. As if to confirm his conclusion, Norbert tells Essola the story of a girl married by force to a rich merchant protected by the colonial authorities. This, he adds, happened before independence. Essola's repetitive question, "comme avant l'indépendance?" ('as before independence?'), and the story of the girl both echo the fate of Perpetua and the leitmotiv "rien n'avait changé" ('nothing had changed') in the novel. The repetition of the same incident and the interrogation of Essola accentuate the theme of the perpetuation of the oppression of women through various times, political regimes, and new generations.

It is unfair, therefore, to suggest that the novelist gives credit to those who condemn Essola for abandoning his family by joining the freedom fighters. Following this analysis, one could only end in a dilemma, the false dilemma of the freedom fighter: the family or the country? Either way, could he ever escape a certain feeling of guilt? A more fruitful line of inquiry lies in the answer to the question, What kind of a novel is *Perpetua*? It is a novel about failure, the failure of a revolution—one that has not achieved the transformation it set out to produce. Herein lies the "mystery" of the neocolonial state. The aborted revolution produced a highly negative transformation that, according to numerous voices in the narrative, seems much worse than the colonial state. The tragedy of history stems from this painfully negative reversal, and the sorrow of Essola is the sorrow of all the dispossessed whose disillusionment is deeply seated (*Perpetua,* p. 195).

In effect, Essola is guilty. But what is he guilty of? It is perhaps correct, as it has been suggested,[11] that he is guilty of contributing to the death of his sister, not by abandoning her to join the freedom fighters, but rather, by failing to bring the necessary social transformation to fruition. This failure, then, is the ultimate crime of the freedom fighter. In the novel, Essola is the only visible veteran freedom fighter. Attached to the character is the dimension of a representative, though now shaky, of the formidable organization once headed by Ruben.

A Shared Responsibility: Will the Defendant Please Rise?

Can the responsibility of the failure of the revolution be placed on Essola solely? Are the Rubenists an irresponsible lot who led their people into their disastrous present condition? Within the narrative, the answer seems to be no, since the actions of Ruben and his organization are honored by the hopeful, but dispossessed, masses of the country. The novel is filled with references that indicate the general preference and support—even if veiled—for the freedom fighters. Although the regime relentlessly seeks not only to discredit them, but also to eliminate them from the collective memory of the people and drop them into the abyss of oblivion, Ruben and his men are seen as heroes.

Responsibility for the overall conditions that create such victims as Perpetua is beyond the power of one person or even a group of persons. The narrative seems to insist on the idea of a shared responsibility, although in varying degrees, in this matter. As in Ngugi's *A Grain of Wheat*, one may ask, "Is there a clean, innocent character in *Perpetua*?"

In one or more ways, it seems that each person, from Ntermelen to Fort-Nègre, is guilty of some fault or some crime against friends, relations, or the nation. Essola is a renegade; he beats his mother and assassinates his brother, actions that open and close the novel. Maria is guilty of selling Perpetua away and, thereafter, abandoning her to the cynical "buyer." She is also guilty of selling Antonia. Maria is guilty of preferring Martin, the "good-for-nothing," to her more vigorous son. Her hatred for Essola reaches the level of death wishes. She is guilty of turning Martin into an incapable man by spoiling him. There are even suggestions of fantasies, on her part, of an incestuous relationship with him. Ultimately, she is the prototype of the insatiable mother who devours her own progeny. While drunk, Martin confesses that he enjoyed giving his sister away so he could spend the money of the bride-wealth on alcohol. Anna-Maria encourages Perpetua to submit to all the demands of Edouard, including to sleep with M'Barg'Onana in order to gain a quick promotion for her husband. Amougou also refuses to get involved, but he encourages Perpetua to marry Edouard, even without a church celebration. Did Zeyang really try to pull Perpetua away on time? It is unclear. Why does he whip the mistress of Edouard? Did she deserve such a punishment from Zeyang? However one looks at it, Zeyang was operating a transfer of anger away from Edouard, who is the guilty one, to a poor unknown prostitute. Crescentia is guilty of adultery while her husband was in detention. Norbert tries to justify himself by arguing that even the hard-core revolutionaries, like the Rubenist freedom fighters, are nowadays joining the regime of the black dictator. Even top officials are not safe. They only harbor a shaky sense of confidence sustained by their brutality and terrorist activities. Everybody is responsible for the general state of degeneration of the nation. It is this sense of shared guilt that Essola throws in Maria's face in the last pages of the novel (*Perpetua*, pp. 212-13). The death of Perpetua amidst general silence or indifference is an echo of the death of Ruben. As in a grim ritual, the nation devours, in the image of Maria the devouring mother, the best of her children. In a sense, the retribution for these crimes is also shared in insecurity, disease, and pervasive violence.

The Symbolic Significance of *Perpetua*

Neither one person (e.g., Essola, Maria, Edouard, or Zeyang) nor a group of persons (e.g., the Rubenists or the dictatorial regime of Baba Toura) alone can be held totally responsible for the state of degeneration of the society that "sacrificed" Perpetua. Of course, the story of Perpetua can be read as a common family tragedy or the consequence of living in a degenerate society. Yet it can also be seen in light of the political explanations offered by Crescentia and, more explicitly, by Stephano. The critics have given a political interpretation of *Perpetua*—sometimes at the expense of the fiction—for a good reason. The narrative lays a particularly heavy emphasis on the political dimension of the social life around Perpetua. For one thing, Essola's return, which triggers the investigation, has political ramifications. He forsakes the struggle that caused him to be jailed, and his return fuels the memories. Those who knew him before his detention seem to remember him as a hard-core Rubenist. They talk to him about the struggle for independence; they also describe independence in its present form as regrettable, if not altogether repugnant. Everybody, including the Greek, Amougou, Martin, Zeyang, Stephano, Norbert, and Crescentia, talks about politics. Essola himself was a political prisoner. The quick promotion of Edouard, the demise of M'Barg'Onana, and the death of Zeyang have political dimensions.

Every major event is narrated with at least two motives: a personal drama and a political confrontation. For example, Edouard and Zeyang are opposed on two levels. On the political level, the two men are on the extreme poles of the political struggle, as Edouard adheres totally to the regime of Baba Toura while Zeyang fights the regime. On the sentimental level, Zeyang succeeds where Edouard fails; Perpetua loves Zeyang, but she remains numb to her husband. Edouard can only keep her by using treachery and force.

Practically, every individual character makes a statement on politics. Thus, Amougou claims that Essola has gained political fame in the country, becoming as fabulous as Akomo in the minds of his people (*Perpetua*, p. 29). Despite his conservative traditional tendency, Amougou draws a compelling picture of the state. In his eyes, the independent country is no less than an authoritarian state, where the police agents enjoy unlimited power to do as they please, plundering the meager revenues of the poor peasants. Amougou is completely disillusioned with independence, which appears even more repressive than colonialism (*Perpetua*, p. 20).

Martin testifies against the state for its persecution of intellectuals. He knows that things might have been different under the leadership of Ruben. But since the country is under the rule of Baba Toura, Martin (the alcoholic brother of the freedom fighter) can only deduce that the intellectuals will continue to be the target of governmental repression. In a sense, the government has already condemned people such as Martin by forcing them to brag about their illiteracy. Although he understands the politics of the government, Martin feels safer displaying ignorance of its nature behind the protective shield of his lack of education. Nevertheless, his comments on the persecution of the intellectuals amount to a condemnation of the new regime.

Even Maria criticizes the corruption of the civil servants in the new regime. She accuses Baba Toura of spoiling everything by bringing independence to a country where things were much better during colonialism.

In addition to these personal testimonies against the independent state, the observations emanating from the narrator take the reader on a tour, so to speak, through the neocolonial institutions. From health care to education, through forestry, the army and the police force, the media, and urbanization, the picture of the state is chaotic. Much like a camera, the eye of the narrator takes the reader through numerous scenes describing the sad state of affairs in the country.

Pregnancy and the prospect of motherhood are initially presented as good news for Perpetua. Even Edouard grows attentive to the needs of his wife. But a visit to the hospital dramatically curbs the optimism of Perpetua. She discovers that health care is a deceitful euphemism in her country. The hospital visit provides the occasion for the narrator to investigate the condition of medical care and how it affects the patients, who are mostly female. Before Perpetua arrives at the hospital, the reader is reminded of the nature of medical care during colonialism. This reminder, in line with the contrastive perspective of the novel, serves the purpose of demonstrating the worsening degradation of the society (*Perpetua*, p. 21).

> At that period, the township had not yet completely lost all recollection of the customs of the colonial regime which, if nothing else, had been a great provider of medical care and welcomed all patients without discrimination. (*Perpetua*, p. 110)

Of all the institutions of this independent state, none is more degrading than the educational system. Its total inefficiency is revealed when Edouard repeatedly takes and fails the test for the police force. After the first test, Edouard comes home to discuss the exam with his friends. Perpetua offers the puzzled group of men a real lesson in French grammar as well as a sound understanding of mathematical problems. In *African Literature in French*,[12] Dorothy S. Blair criticizes Beti because

> He puts a long, pedantic lesson in French grammar into the mouth of the fifteen-year-old Perpetua, fresh from her convent school, which does not endear the bride of three months to her less erudite and slower-witted husband. *Nor does the reader find these pages lifted direct from a grammar manual, particularly palatable in a novel.* (My emphasis)

If Perpetua's discourse sounds like a grammar book, it does have the advantage of depicting realistically the language training she received in school. French, it appears, is the alcoholism of the intellectuals. On the other hand, African languages are ignored by the educational system, and their usage is often forbidden in schools. It is this compelling reality that the episode about Edouard's exams highlights in the novel. The episode also revitalizes the narrative by revealing Edouard's renewed hatred for Perpetua for daring to display her superior intelligence. The woman succeeds brilliantly where the man fails, and Edouard feels humiliated by this.

It should be noted that there are two parts to the police force exam: grammar and math. The questions in each are carefully chosen. The math question is about the resolution of a financial problem. The prospective investor is a modest second-grade civil servant, like Edouard, who intends to buy a motorcycle. Considering his meager salary, what are his alternatives? The test is labeled "economics," and the label insidiously echoes and amplifies a political campaign designed to make people think that the difficulties of the state can only be solved by a "good understanding"— not necessarily practice—of economics. The people sarcastically refer to the campaign, calling it "economitis" or "economyth," emphasizing its unhealthy nature and its unrealistic character. Once again, Essola recognizes in this campaign a pattern already established during colonialism, when Africans were geared toward studying elementary rules of agriculture as the sole rewarding enterprise for them. Now, the French language and "economics" are presented as the magic words that create prosperity.

The economics test echoes another event that affects Edouard in the novel. His fight with Caracalla, a more successful former schoolmate, originates from the latter's wisdom in saving to purchase a motorcycle. Caracalla does this in the fashion described by Perpetua and Jean Dupont as the sensible solution of the economics test. Of course, the anger of Edouard stems more directly from his jealousy and the fact that Caracalla reminds him of Perpetua's superior intelligence. Nevertheless, the motorcycle purchase introduces the dispute. There is also a political dispute between the two men, since Caracalla makes a point of telling Edouard that he is a mere bootlicker of "his excellency" Baba Toura, the dictator.

That the country suffers from an economic disease is apparent from the beginning of the novel. But it is during the meeting of Stephano, Zeyang, and Essola that the reader "hears" an impassioned exchange detailing the irresponsible methods of exploitation of the country's resources under the regime of Baba Toura. The disappearance of local handicraft production and the wasteful exploitation of natural resources, especially wood, form the basis of Stephano's and Zeyang's condemnation of the economic policies of the regime. They also maintain that the lack of urban planning and the inefficiency of the media accentuate the economic and cultural chaos of the state.

Contrast is a major narrative technique in *Perpetua*. The time of the narration is constantly contrasted and compared with the past, with the era of colonial rule in the nameless African state that forms the geographic and social background of *Perpetua*. Contrast is shown at the levels of individual events and collective history. It starts in the country as Essola returns home; it continues in the urban areas; it is pursued through an "investigation" of various state institutions; and finally, it culminates in parricide, the dislocation of family ties, and the second, perhaps final, departure of Essola from home.

Perpetua deals with the perpetuation of old evils. It insists that the present cannot be fully understood without taking the past into account. Thus, it also suggests that the causes of the present state of social degeneration are embedded in the history of the colonial state. Throughout the novel, independence is generally regarded as an odd euphemism because the independent state is more dependent today on the former colonial power than it was during colonialism.

The relationship between the two entities is portrayed through the presence of the former colonial administrators who remain in powerful political positions. They appear to be the real decision makers, hidden and protected by African front men. The government structure of the independent state itself is a reflection of the relationship between the former colonial power and the regime of Baba Toura. The structure rests on a double frame made of African politicians and civil servants, and French counselors.

The novel focuses on the relations of dependency between the African state and France. The social science studies of the 1970s placed particular emphasis on the unequal nature of these relations. It is safe to say that Beti is a writer of his time who pays close attention to new developments. The notion that dependency is a universal feature that cannot be a cause of economic distress in the Third World has lingered around in some Western and Third World quarters. But as Walter Rodney points out, dependency should not be confused with interdependency, for the dependency of a former colony, now constitutionally independent, on the metropolitan country is underscored by domination.[13]

By linking the "new" state to the colonial state, by insisting on the political nature of the prevailing social conditions, by emphasizing the perpetuation and worsening of old evils in the present within a largely political narrative framework, Beti successfully captures the spirit of an era. The novelist focuses on the description of a system. With the acute sense of observation that already appears in his anticolonial novels, he is able to show that neocolonialism is also a well-constructed system that extends colonialism into the present. The fact that the novel describes neocolonialism while dismantling the myth of independence is more strongly symbolized in references to Kwameh Nkrumah, former president of Ghana (*Perpetua*, p. 231). Of all the Third World statesmen, none to my knowledge has studied and described neocolonialism as a system more eloquently than Nkrumah.[14] Thus, historical references in Beti's novels are carefully chosen.

Perpetua is a testimony on the times by one of Africa's most attentive and talented novelists. For this reason, Beti uses a significant quotation at the beginning of the book. It is a short excerpt from chapter nineteen of *Candide,* where Voltaire describes the conditions of black slaves in the Caribbean; the widely anthologized passage is best known as "Le Nègre de Surinam."

> Our only clothing is a pair of linen pants, which we are given twice a year. When we work at the sugar mill, if a finger gets caught in the millstone, they cut off our whole hand. When we try to run away, they cut off our leg. This is the price that has to be paid so that you can eat sugar in Europe.[15]

As far as the novel describes neocolonialism, a system that plagues most African countries, *Perpetua* symbolizes Africa. The universalization of the symbol is suggested in the narrative by parallel descriptions of Perpetua's individual history on the one hand, and the degradation of social life on the other. It is fairly easy, for example, to establish a correlation between the exploitation of the helpless and weak Perpetua and the exploitation of a defenseless Africa. Maria, the devouring mother, sells her daughters away as Baba Toura sells the resources of his country. Maria wastes the money by letting her alcoholic son spend it on more alcohol, as some African politicians and businessmen indulge in conspicuous consumption instead of sound investments. Baba Toura "begets" Edouard, and Ruben "begets" Abena and Mor-Zamba in *Remember Ruben.* While Baba Toura is given the nickname "Black Nero," Edouard is described as the "replica of Baba Toura in Zombotown," "a miniature Baba Toura" (*Perpetua,* pp. 249-50).

Perpetua is the story of a humble, intelligent, and loving young woman. She is a victim, one among many, of a society where life is so precarious, so cheap, that mothers sell their daughters, brothers abandon their sisters, parricide takes place, and jealousy, bitterness, and misery prevail. It is "Sodom and Gomorrah" reinvented altogether. *Perpetua* is a tragic novel. It is the story of a domestic tragedy; in the end, Maria's family is broken, two of her children dead, the other two gone. A murder (Martin), an execution (Zeyang), and a long and horrible social, as well as physical, agony (Perpetua) seal the novel into the vicious circle of an almost ritual, but futile, manslaughter. It is the chronicle of a historical tragedy about the transformation of a poor, yet hopeful, society into an almost hopeless one, where one form of brutal rule calls for a more advanced form of degradation. The condition of the poor people is best described—this is apparently unintended by the narrator—in the excerpt from the dictation given during Edouard's exam. Perpetua is the only one who understands the sentence and grasps its grammatical complexity. The sentence eloquently speaks of the condition in which her fellow citizens live.

> Flocking from every province of the kingdom, the poor folk who claimed no more than the means of subsistence heard themselves called upon not to appear in the sight of their sovereign. (*Perpetua,* pp. 88-89)

Above all, *Perpetua* may be seen as a feminist novel. Unlike other novels of pessimistic tendencies, it emphasizes the social condition of African women and illustrates the position of second-class citizens, where they are relegated. The African woman symbolized in Perpetua must endure polygamy and bear children in a futile birth and death ritual. Her life is disposed of by the men and elders in spite of her efforts; she is used and abused mercilessly. The condition of the African woman also is treated in the historical and contrastive modes. At the end of the novel, Norbert tells a story that is similar to the story of Perpetua but happened during colonialism. The theme of the "habit of unhappiness" is thus established in its temporal dimension.

It is at this level of general representation that the novel suffers a weakness. If, as it has been stated, Perpetua symbolizes the African woman, then Beti has overstated the case and created a "cardboard character." After all, Perpetua is a pure victim, weak and totally unfit to survive in her society. But it must be said to Beti's credit that Perpetua is contrasted with other women in the novel. Antonia and Crescentia are of a different caliber. They fight for survival and, indeed, manage to stay afloat in the ocean of evil of their society. Perhaps for this reason, instead of foreshadowing the fate of this pure innocent victim from the beginning of the novel, Beti choose to present her as dead when the novel opens. This choice removes the presumably trying task of dealing directly with Perpetua and allows the novelist to focus on other interesting subjects through the investigation of Essola. Perpetua, it would appear, represents the African woman as a defenseless victim. Crescentia, and to some degree Antonia, represent the burgeoning new African woman who emerges in *Lament*. In the last novel of the trilogy, the role of the women in the revolutionary transformation of Ekoundoum is crucial. They are led by Ngwane-Eligui the Younger, the woman freedom fighter.

Nevertheless, it should be noted that in the absence of the black messiah (Ruben), and even during the bloody reign of the "Black Nero" (Baba Toura), hope survives and dreams are kept alive. Even among the zombies of Zombotown, many characters in the novel continue to carry a dimly lit torch. The veiled reference to the myth of the zombie becomes important in the novel for it speaks of the struggle of the alienated person to regain his consciousness and power of creativity. René Depestre defines the zombie as the colonized, alienated person who should seek out the revitalizing grain of salt.

> Le Zombi, c'est l'homme colonisé, aliéné, l'homme qui a perdu sa raison et son esprit et qui est devenu une simple force de travail. Et dans ce mythe, il est dit qu'il ne faut pas donner du sel au zombi, parce qu'il retrouverait, par le sel, sa conscience et son imagination.
>
> Donc, nous devons tous voler le sel, même s'il faut aller le chercher dans la culture occidentale. Du sel, pour notre maison, pour notre imagination, afin que le zombi qui existe en chacun de

nous puisse se réveiller et faire un usage dynamique de son
imagination pour que la révolution triomphe.[16]

> *The zombie is the colonized, alienated man, the man who has
> lost his reason and his spirit and who has become a simple
> working force. And in this myth, it is said that one must not give
> salt to the zombie, because by taking salt, he would recover his
> consciousness and his imagination.*
> *Therefore, we must all steal this salt, even if we have to seek
> it in Western culture. Salt for our home, for our imagination, so
> that the zombie who exists in each one of us can awaken and
> actively use his imagination in order that the revolution may
> triumph.* (My translation)

In Zombotown, there are also salt-seekers. Characters like Zeyang,
Stephano, Anna-Maria, Crescentia, and Jean Dupont do try to confront the
regime. They fail, but they keep the hope alive in the people around them
by giving them a sense of dignity and pride. *Perpetua* remains the negative
transformation of *Remember Ruben*. Antithetical to the generally active and
hopeful spirit of the first novel of the trilogy, *Perpetua* is tragically gloomy,
formally complex, and violent. The hope and creativity that are so strongly
stifled in *Perpetua* will germinate and blossom in *Lament*.

*Lament for an African Pol*_____

The Positive Transformation

Lament for an African Pol is the continuation of *Remember Ruben*.
With the exception of the young Evariste, the two main characters are both
familiar figures. The reverse symmetry projected in *Remember Ruben* is
carried out in this novel. Similarly, the action that unfolds in *Lament* was
announced in *Remember Ruben*. The battle that ends *Remember Ruben*
energizes the beginning of this novel and propels it into an action-packed
saga, thus turning *Lament* into a giant firework that illuminates Ekoundoum
with infinite pieces of light.

The reader is confronted with a solemn metamorphosis of the subject
while a radical social transformation takes place in Ekoundoum. This
transfiguration of the subject is already prophesied at the beginning of
the novel:

> new fireworks doubtless will explode elsewhere, far from Kola-
> Kola, to illuminate the long night that Hurricane-Viet had predicted
> as one result of Ruben's disappearance. (*Lament*, p. 22)

However, this transformation is only possible through the efforts of the
Rubenists and in a popular armed insurrection against the despot chief. If
Perpetua marks the descent of the subject in hell, *Lament* elevates it and
glorifies it. It is a movement upward, marked by social and psychological

transformations. The trilogy progresses from alienation, temporary exile in *Remember Ruben*, and tragic social degradation in *Perpetua*, to armed insurrection against despotism and radical social transformation. At the end of *Lament*, the subject is completely transfigured, enlightened and blooming, although it is not totally devoid of potential trouble.

Lament is the novel in the trilogy that dramatizes the advent of qualitative changes. Ekoundoum, the world of *Remember Ruben*, undergoes a total transformation that affects life in its multiple facets and permeates everything. In the narrative, these transformations transpire through the social fabric, its relations, and its structures; also, the changes transpire through mental and physical attitudes. The narrator's voice now is more harmonious, even if occasionally hesitant or laughing. It remains confident, knowing, and vigorous. The tone is generally enthusiastic, passionately captivating. If the reader is mesmerized and seduced throughout the adventure by these aspects of the narrative, it is primarily because *Lament* is the birthplace of a new being, a new society. The dynamism that animates the work is partly due to the final convulsions of this long birth process. Prophecies made a long time ago in *Remember Ruben* and hidden desires felt in *Perpetua* take on concrete forms and are now being fulfilled in *Lament*. The characters hardly realize the significance of the events as fulfillment of prophecies. But the narrator, telling the story in retrospect and from the vantage point of the present (the time of narration), can now see the hidden relationship. Herein lies an important part of his confidence and unfailing optimism. It becomes clear that the entire trilogy is the expression of a myth-making effort. This appears not only in the fulfillment of the difficult but successful journey of the subject to Ekoundoum, but also in the symbolism associated with the events of the journey. After a brief consideration of time and space in *Lament*, the following discussion focuses on the various types of transformations that occur in it.

Time and Space in *Lament*

The story is the unfolding of the reverse symmetry of *Remember Ruben*, where Mor-Zamba goes from Ekoundoum to Fort-Nègre. In *Lament*, he goes from the city to the country. Traveling mostly on foot and by night, the Rubenists are forced to make many stops on their long journey to Ekoundoum. This movement allows them to learn more about the country, engaging in minor battles that prepare them for the final confrontation in Ekoundoum. The long march is both a lesson in geography and sociology, as well as a test of endurance, for the guerrillas.

At the symbolic level, and as an extension of the previous novels, *Lament* covers a larger world. Bernard Mouralis has observed that the narrative can be understood as the example of an experience that could be extended to the entire nation. This is particularly true as the physical setting of Ekoundoum becomes reminiscent of the structure of the colonial city in its Manichean division. Ultimately, the narrative associates all of Africa with the vision it proposes.

> Once past Saneongo, the perceptive traveler had the impression, even at night in the darkness, of having finally embraced the very soul of the young Republic, as if it were a woman who had remained away far too long, and beyond it, perhaps, that of Africa itself. (*Lament*, p. 22)

In contrast with *Remember Ruben*, the plot unfolds rapidly in one year, from January 1960 to January 1961. Perhaps the most important aspect of time in *Lament* is found in its frame of night/day duality. The Rubenists travel mostly by night. The night symbolizes uncertainty, but it also protects the guerrillas. When the night is affected by the moon, as in part two, it evokes a positive image associated with the involvement of the women in the insurrection against the chief. The sun is sometimes associated with danger but more often with glory; the transformations announcing a new era that occur in the last part of the novel are described in terms of sunshine.

The Transformations

The transformations that occur in Ekoundoum can be grouped in three broad categories that are linked together in the narrative. There are individual, collective, and institutional transformations.

Individual Transformations

Individual transformations affect the characters in the novel. Once inside the forest, Mor-Zamba undergoes a complete metamorphosis generated by his rediscovery of a familiar environment. His response to the surroundings testifies to the authencity of the experience (*Lament*, pp. 79-80). Toward the end of the book, Mor-Zamba is implicitly accepted as the city's new leader. His companions feel this transformation of "the lion of Kola-Kola" (*Lament*, p. 272).

Mor-Kinda also is transformed in the change from city to country from the old mischievous houseboy of Sandrinelli into an accomplished freedom fighter. In the course of the struggle, he learns that if the gun— i.e., violence—is a necessary means for liberation, the goal of the freedom fighter remains the celebration of life, not ritualistic bloodshed. Like Mor-Zamba, he verbalizes his awareness of his own transformation.

> You might not believe it, Bumpkin, but since I met Hurricane-Viet, I'm no longer the same person. (*Lament*, p. 83)

Meanwhile, Evariste, the youngest of the trio, grows from a bookish collegian into an officer of the freedom fighters.

In Ekoundoum, Ngwane-Eligui the Younger gives the most support to the liberation effort. A captive in the palace of the chief, she seeks to organize women against their common oppressor. Ngwane-Eligui the Younger defiantly takes her freedom, organizes women to free more women, and becomes a leader of freedom fighters. She is considered "the very soul of the insurrection," as well as a major advocate of institutional transformations.

Even Mor-Bita, the old despot, undergoes a mental transformation. Nearly on his deathbed, he confesses to Mor-Kinda, rebels against the missionaries, and asks them to leave the city so as not to interfere any longer in the internal affairs of his people. Thus, shortly before his death, he surrenders to the will of the people of Ekoundoum.

Father Van den Rietter also regains some insight as he is forced by events to rediscover his religious role. He learns to stop meddling in the affairs of the chief and the citizens of Ekoundoum, resuming with humility his church activities (*Lament*, p. 291). But the transformation happens too late. Van den Rietter is expelled from Ekoundoum and soon dies in the neighboring "country of the English." His role is assumed by Brother Nicholas, who is instructed to supervise the construction of hospitals and schools. Henceforth, the activities of the priest will unfold in the church and in the field, in the service of his followers, not against them.

Collective Transformations

They affect everybody, from the family of the chief and the women of the *sixa*,[17] to the youth. This stage is best described as the liberation stage in the narrative. Successive events bring about decisive confrontations liberating segments of society in the process. It is important to keep in mind that the individual transformations are a function of the combined effects of situation, goal, and means. But in turn, the individual transformations affect the course of the pursued collective transformations.

The collective transformations start with the women. The mothers take the first action toward their liberation by seeking to save their children from the sudden epidemic fever that has plunged the city into great despair. Led by Ngwane-Eligui The Younger, they send their daughters on the trails of the Rubenists. While Mor-Zamba provides health care to their children, the women offer protection to the Rubenists. To get to them, the mothers swear, the guards of the old despot will have to walk over their dead bodies. The female elders set out to build a wall around the "hospital." In the course of the day, more women join the workers—some providing food, some nursing the children—all of them working in a spirit of togetherness. In contrast with Maria, the devouring mother of Perpetua, these mothers care about, and fight for the survival of, their children.

The arrival of "the prisoners of the mission" from the seclusion of the *sixa* brings out the atmosphere of insurrection smoldering amongst the women. The *sixa* women win their freedom through a violent rebellion against their custodians. The participation of the mulatto girl, niece of Brother Nicholas, and the effort of the women announce the irreversibility of their liberation. But this event is only the initial phase in the collective transformations occurring in Ekoundoum.

The narrative shifts to the male citizens. Their liberation originates in the most glorified single event of the novel: the confrontation between Father Van den Rietter and Mor-Kinda. It is a battle of skill where Van den Rietter is defeated at his own game. He appears menacingly in the midst of the rebellious women, holding a small handgun. Seeking to frighten the men, he shoots and kills four flying eagles. But the effect of surprise he sought is reversed as Mor-Kinda steps out with a gun, stands by the Catholic priest, and shoots and kills an eagle. Mor-Kinda's act is described as the beginning of a new era (*Lament*, p. 306).

This memorable action liberates the young men from their fear of the authoritarian priest who is now completely desacralized and demystified. They regain a sense of pride and disarm the priest. Even the little boys express joy at the new prospect of hunting freely on the land without fear of reprisals from the guards (*Lament*, p. 308).

The wives of the chief, who were forced to stay with the impotent despot, rebel against their unjust condition. Led by Ngwane-Eligui The Younger, they leave the dying chief. The rebellion is followed by the "confessions of the women," who publicly denounce the false "father of the nation" and reveal the identities of their real lovers and the real fathers of the so-called "children of the chief." They now can marry the men they truly love. In the process, all the children of the chief discover, like Mor-Zamba, their true identities as rightful members of the city of Ekoundoum.

Institutional Transformations

Institutional transformations affect the laws of society, especially some traditions that appear impractical or unjust. The public "confessions of the women," for example, result in banning the tradition that allows parents to negotiate the marriages of their offspring without consulting the proposed couple. This practice, the reader recalls, sealed the fate of Perpetua. Also, it is decided that polygamy will no longer be the rule in Ekoundoum. These revolutionary transformations occur as a result of the meeting during which the women debate the problem of polygamy and take a firm stand against the practice.

Transformation also occurs in the church, which is represented by two apostles: a white messenger to announce the coming of Christ, the white messiah, and a black messenger to announce the coming of Abena, the black messiah. This consensus is reached after the intervention of an elderly woman following the speech by Mor-Zamba, who sought the immediate dismissal of the missionaries at the Christmas midnight mass (*Lament*, p. 334).

A major social transformation appears in the new regulations concerning the land that had been appropriated by the old despot. The land will now be distributed to the peasants. This decision eliminates the slave labor force created and developed by the chief and Van den Rietter for their own plantations. The unmarried women are the first ones to test this new rule. They create the first self-help style communal farms. The reader finds in these changes a transformation of the quality of labor itself from slave labor to a collective, independent, self-help work organization.

To insure that these transformations are respected by all, and to dispel the danger of a coup from the chief and the missionaries, Mor-Kinda organizes a popular militia recruited from his young followers.

These are some of the institutional transformations that occur in Ekoundoum. Mor-Zamba, the new, yet undeclared, leader becomes the tireless negotiator between the various interest groups that form the new community. He is constantly shuttling from Mor-Kinda and his companions to the counsel of elders and back to the women's group. He is forced, at times, to use his authority to remind the youth (Mor-Kinda and Ngwane-Eligui The Younger) that developments in the city need to be carried out in a democratic fashion, that issues should be discussed openly and understood by everyone, and that everyone should take part in the decision-making process. Incidentally, this firm attachment of Mor-Zamba to the democratic ideal of establishing a popular authority causes the first major rift between him and his younger friends who favor more expedient methods.

The transformations categorized above are, of course, interlinked in a more complex network within the narrative. Nevertheless, the insurrectional phase of the narrative lays a particularly heavy emphasis on the transformational process of Ekoundoum. The reader should consider the symbolical dimension of Ekoundoum, seen as a microcosm of a wider region, in order to appreciate the revolutionary importance of the narrative. *Lament* is not only the first novel that describes, however symbolically, a guerrilla warfare in West Africa, it also focuses on the description of a social transformation process. The development of this process in the novel generates a new vision. This vision of transformations is energized and propelled into the world of the possible and desirable by the narrative. It should be noted that most of the transformations developed in the novel have been attempted already in real life inside and outside Africa: land reforms, popular militia, family laws concerning marriage, polygamy, and religious transformations, to mention a few.

Above all, the novel reiterates Beti's tireless plea for freedom of expression, the reestablishment of a true spirit of palaver and debates, especially around public issues that appear controversial. Of all the African traditions he discusses, Beti finds this democratic institution of public debate more appealing, an aspect of African culture that he is very proud of.

It becomes obvious that what *Lament* embodies is the infinitely complex process of changing oneself, of moving toward a total transformation of the subject, for a wholesome metamorphosis. The emphasis is placed on the active subject, what it does and does not do in order to experience this process successfully. It is a collective process of psychological transformation and adaptability to new situations. Beti confirms this in an interview in which he defines his understanding of the concept of progress:

> Je suis partisan du progrès, pas forcément du progrès technique. Le progrès technique ne veut rien dire. Ce qui compte le plus, c'est le progrès des psychologies, le progrès du groupe, la faculté qu'a le groupe de s'adapter à une situation nouvelle. C'est ça le progrès pour moi.[18]

> *I am for progress, not necessarily technical progress. Technical progress does not mean anything. What counts the most of all is the progress of the psychologies, the progress of the group, the ability of the group to adapt itself to a new situation. That, to me, is progress.* (My translation)

Notes 3

[1] Hassan el Nouty, "Anatomie de Remember Ruben" (Paper presented at the African Literature Association Annual Conference, Clairemont, Calif., April 1981), 5.

[2] Martin T. Bestman, "Structure du récit et mécanique de l'action révolutionnaire dans Remember Ruben," *Présence Francophone*, no. 23 (1981): 63.

[3] Ibid., 76.

[4] Gerald Moore, *Twelve African Writers* (Bloomington: Indiana University Press, 1980), 210.

[5] el Nouty, "Anatomie," 9.

[6] Eloise A. Brière, "*Remember Ruben*: Etude spatio-temporelle," *Présence Francophone*, no. 15 (1977), 35.

[7] Ibid., 36-37.

[8] Eza Boto, *Ville cruelle* (Paris: Présence Africaine, 1953), 24.

[9] Ayi Kwei Armah, *The Beautyful Ones Are Not Yet Born* (London: Heinemann, 1969); Ahmadou Kourouma, *Les Soleils des indépendances* (Paris: Seuil, 1970); and Alioune Fantoure, *Le Cercle des Tropiques* (Paris: Présence Africaine, 1972).

[10] For a study of time in *Perpetua*, see Bernard Mouralis's "Aspects de l'écriture dans *Perpétue et l'habitude du malheur* de Mongo Béti," *Présence Francophone*, no. 17 (1978): 45-68, and *Comprendre L'oeuvre de Mongo Béti* (Paris: Editions Saint Paul, 1981).

[11] See Mouralis, *Comprendre,* and Bestman, "Structure du recit."

[12] Dorothy S. Blair, *African Literature in French* (Cambridge: Cambridge University Press, 1976), 284.

[13] Walter Rodney, "Problems of Third World Development," *Ufahamu* 3, no. 2 (Fall 1972): 46; reprinted in *Ufahamu* 11, no. 1 (Summer 1981): 115-32.

[14] Kwameh Nkrumah, *Neo-colonialism, the Last Stage of Imperialism* (London: Heinemann, 1965).

[15] Voltaire, *Candide,* in *Romans et contes.* (Paris: Garnier-Flammarion, 1966), 222.

[16] "Pour une mutation globale," interview with René Depestre, *Poésie,* nos. 43-45 (January-June 1976): 86.

[17] "In every mission in the southern Cameroun there is a building which houses, in principle, all the young girls engaged to be married. This is the *sixa*. All our girls who want to be married in the strict Catholic was must stay in the *sixa* for two to four months, except in special cases, which are always numerous. The defenders of this institution praise its usefulness, if not its necessity. Doesn't it prepare these girls to be mothers of Christian families? But this justification is disputed by others. What is

certain is that the inmates of the *sixa* are compelled to do manual labor for more than ten hours every day." Mongo Beti, *The Poor Christ of Bomba* (London: Heinemann, 1971), 5.

[18] Anthony Biakolo, "Entretien avec Mongo Beti," *Peuples Noirs/Peuples Africains,* no. 10 (July-August 1979): 110-11.

4

The Odyssey
Social Transformations in the Mau Mau Trilogy

Introduction

Chapter two of this book outlines the mythic foundation of Ngugi's trilogy of the African quest for freedom. It shows that the land issue is central to his narrative and suggests that there is a historical correlation—not obvious to the characters—between Ngotho's teleological view of history and the actual struggle of the trilogy in which Boro, his son, plays an important role.

Ngotho, the peasant whose piece of land has been expropriated, is a man of faith. He remains faithful to the prophecy of Mugo wa Kibiro, a visionary who foretold the return of the lost land to the Gikuyu people. Yet, Ngotho does very little to bring this prophecy to realization. On the contrary, he believes it his responsibility to "stick around," working for Howlands on the land that belonged to his father and waiting for the coming of the black messiah. Not until later on is Ngotho drawn closer to action. Boro rebels against his father's attitude. Having rejected his father's position, Boro rebels against the cruel exploitation of the landless peasants by joining the Land and Freedom Army, which advocates armed struggle. He takes their oath and joins the freedom fighters in the forest. Thus, he unwittingly helps to actualize the prophecy by engaging in the battle for the land. Here, the whole narrative strains to register the fulfillment of the quest for freedom that is linked to the land. The quest is also the occasion for a chronicle of the past and the present, as well as the occasion for the novelist to propose a vision of future social transformations in his trilogy. Father and son, Ngotho and Boro, both share the aspiration without sharing the background premises. Historical realism and visionary outlook are permanent features of Ngugi's work.

The trilogy chronicles the quest for freedom by depicting the successive social and psychological transformations that occur as a result of the various social conflicts. What Boro symbolizes in the novel is the odyssey of generations of Gikuyus toward freedom, toward the realization of the prophecy.

This chapter shows the various types of transformations that occur in the trilogy as it chronicles a movement toward Uhuru. The landless and poor citizens that comprise the majority of the characters constitute the core of the subject of the fictionalized quest. This subject evolves from being a passive acceptor of colonial society to an active challenger of the system. As it regains a higher level of freedom, it must face numerous and complex transformations brought about by the violent turmoil arising from its quest. In the light of the Mau Mau revolution, the subject of the odyssey casts a critical look at its own body and at the trail left behind, in order to assess the quality of the transformations. New problems have emerged from the transformation brought about during the odyssey. On the day of Uhuru, the reader knows that a new society is born, but also that it is not yet free.

One of the major features of the new society is its social class orientation. During the odyssey, classes slowly emerge as a new source of social confrontations. This theme is sketched in *Weep Not, Child*, developed in *A Grain of Wheat*, and given full treatment in *Petals of Blood*.

Sowing a Grain of Wheat

Weep Not, Child is a warning signal. It foreshadows *A Grain of Wheat*, which is a more complex and violent novel. *Weep Not, Child* offers strength and faith in place of despair, despite the fact that its violent atmosphere conveys a sense of chaos and disorder. The child should remain strong because a grain is being sown that will hopefully germinate to produce wheat. This optimistic prospect is not meant to justify such violence as Howlands's. There is no vengeful smile from the prophet at the prospect of sowing a grain. The novel simply marvels at the possibility of a new order. What it will bring no one knows yet, but the general perspective is one of optimism against the background of the present condition. The sowing of the grain constitutes a major moment of the odyssey. It creates momentous transformations at the collective level and in the individual lives of the characters.

Collective Transformations

The collective transformations affect the environment and the society at large in form and in substance. The transformation that affects the environment is a rather negative one. It comes in the form of a destructive drought and chaos arising from the war. The contrast between the images of the environment then and after the State of Emergency is striking. The richness and luxuriance of the region is described in the first part of *A Grain of Wheat*. In those days, "it was quiet and cool in Kinenie Forest," a place of frolicsome, youthful, and romantic encounters, of music and dance, of joy and love. But even then, the signs of future turmoil loomed in the horizon.

> Kihika and Wambuku found an open place in the sun. The thick part of the forest, the dancers in the wood, and the hungry eyes of Njeri were behind them. Here green wattle trees and bush sloped steeply into the valley below. The valley sprawled flat for a distance and then bounced into a ridge of small hills. Beyond and to the right, Kihika could just trace the outlines of Mahee Police Station, a symbol of that might which dominated Kenya to the door of every hut. (*Grain*, p. 111)

It was on the edge of the same Kinenie Forest that Kihika was caught and hanged. The forest becomes a fearsome place where violence and death replace romantic encounters.

The towns of Thabai and Rung'ei are equally affected by the State of Emergency. Before the declaration, both communities had a robust economy, with Indians and Africans free to compete for customers. But the war puts an end to trade, destroying most of the booming economic life of the area. At the end of the Emergency, both towns changed radically. On his return from the Yala Detention Camp, Gikonyo discovers two strange towns.

> He went out of the hut—how it reeked with smoke—and wandered through the new Thabai village where one street led into another and dust trailed behind at his heels. The very air choked him; Thabai was just another detention camp; would he ever get out of it? But to go where? He followed the tarmac road which led him into Rung'ei. The Indian shops had been moved into a new center; the tall buildings were made of stones; electric lights and tarmac streets made the place appear as a slice of the big city. The sewage smelt; it had not been cleaned for a year. He went on and came to the African shops in Rung'ei; they were all closed; tall grass and wild bush clambered around the walls of the rusty buildings and covered the ground that was once the market-place. Most of the buildings had battered walls with large gaping holes, smashed and splintered doors that stared at him—ruins that gave only hints of an earlier civilization. At the door of one building, Gikonyo picked up a broken plank; the fading letters on it, capitals, had lost their legs and hands but after careful scrutiny he made out the word HOTEL. Inside was a mound of soil; bits of broken china, saucers and glasses were scattered on top. He topped, pecked and poked the wall with the sharp end of the broken plank; suddenly cement and soil tumbled down, in increasing quantity, it seemed the wall would break and fall. Gikonyo rushed out, afraid of the building, of ghost-ridden Rung'ei and did not stop running until he entered the fields. (*Grain*, p. 135)

Images of death and decay abound in the foregoing passage. This quotation is an example of Ngugi's descriptive style at its best. Through his compositional technique, his register of expressions, and his judicious choice of words, he successfully conveys the image of a wasteland. How did Thabai, a sprawling lively little town become "just another detention camp"? Mumbi describes the origins and process of the transformation. In retaliation for a Mau Mau attack against the Mahee Police Post, colonial authorities decide to burn Thabai and to move it to another setting that would be made impregnable. Not only are the people forced to watch their houses burn, they are made to build new ones. Officials also compel them to dig a trench around the new site. In the narrative, images of people collectively taken to and from the trench eloquently echo similar crowd scenes of the detention camps. The women who are left in Thabai carry the brunt of this savage retaliation. Rounded up like animals, they are forced to work from dawn to dusk and then left, by way of deliberate starvation, to the mercy of the Homeguards. Thabai's atmosphere of detention camp is compounded by a high death rate among the "detainees." "All together, twenty-one men and women died" (*Grain*, p. 166) Indeed, those who stayed in Thabai were essentially detainees, especially since they had to carry a passbook to move from the Reserve to the European farms, to work for the Europeans, or simply to move from one location to another. Gikonyo is not alone in his condition. He is a part of the society that, in its entirety, underwent a total transformation. This fact is corroborated by changes occurring within social groups, particularly the youth and the women, the children and the elders.

As the war breaks out, the young men of Thabai who have not joined the freedom fighters hold discretely together, fearing repression.

> He [Gikonyo] went on with the workshop, Karanja and others collected there in the evening, hurled curses and defiance in the air, and received with pride, the personal histories of the latest men to join Kihika. (*Grain*, p. 119)

Their fear and agony are justified, for the colonial government increases the level of repression.

> More men were rounded up and taken to concentration camps— named detention camps for the world outside Kenya. The platform at the railway station was now always empty; girls pined for their lovers behind cold huts and prayed that they would come back from the forest or from the camps. (*Grain*, p. 119)

The old people and the crippled, who cannot work in the trench, are forced to sit and watch their wives and children endure the colonial whip. Women carry the burden of feeding and sheltering the old and the children. To do so, they must also go through the humiliation of prostituting themselves for their merciless masters.

The transformation involves everybody in the community, even men like Karanja, the renegade who betrayed the oath or who never took one. Indeed, the procolonialist Africans are seriously affected by the war.

Karanja becomes a prominent collaborator, a Homeguard, while Mugo receives the ironic retribution of punishment for selling Kihika to the colonial forces.

As shown earlier, the war affects the British community. Robson, a district officer, is a ruthless murderer in uniform. Beyond the particular cases of transformations is the overwhelming sense among the British that the end of their privileges is imminent. They face the possibility of paying for their crimes. The Europeans become dominated by fear and frustration.

Thus, the entire colonial society is deeply affected by the Mau Mau war. All communities bear the scars of the event. Their particular wounds are captured in vivid tableaux in a "yesterday-today" perspective. The tableaux represent images of a general process of social transformation.

Through the detainees, the narrator uses flashbacks and incorporates a "yesterday-today" perspective in the novel. Yesterday, Thabai was a lovely and peaceful town; Rung'ei was a booming commercial center. Today, New Thabai bears the scars of a detention camp, and Rung'ei only exhibits the ghost of its lively past in the nostalgic eyes of Gikonyo. This negative transformation of the environment is caused by the war.

The great stride, the overriding transformation of Kenya, is encapsulated in her passage from colonialism to Uhuru. Independence offers the Africans a taste of the fruit of freedom. But the fruit is sour, for Kenya passes from the hands of European landlords to African landlords. In general terms, the transformation of Kenya is both positive and negative. Indeed, the peasants "who fought the British yet who now see all that they fought for being put on one side," (*Grain*, p. vi) constantly question the official meaning of Uhuru. Independence for whom? Gikonyo discovers that there is a new landlord, an African landlord.

> Following yesterday's talk with the M.P., Gikonyo called on the five men concerned with the scheme. They reviewed their position and decided to enlarge the land company, raise the price per shares. In this war, they would raise enough money for Burton's farm. In the afternoon they went to see Mr. Burton, to see if he would accept a large, first installment. Then they would pay the rest at the end of the month. If the loan promised by the M.P. came, they would use it to develop the farm. The first thing they saw at the main entrance to Green Hill Farms (as Mr. Burton's farm was called) was a signpost. Gikonyo could not believe his eyes when he read the name. They walked to the house without a whisper among themselves, but all dwelling on the same thought. Mr. Burton had left Kenya for England. The new landowner was their own M.P. (*Grain*, pp. 191-92).

It should be said that Ngugi is a talented writer who is able to harmoniously incorporate within large collective tableaux the numerous individual pictures of the psychological and physical transformations of the various characters. The personalities of the characters—including minor ones like Gatu—are rendered with jewel-like minute precision.

Structural Organization of *A Grain of Wheat*

Ngugi's concern for precision and harmony appears in the organization of the narrative. The novel is divided into four parts, each preceded by a quotation from the Bible. Part one is composed of three chapters, while each of the remaining parts contains four chapters.

Both Beti's and Ngugi's novels are informed by the same kind of contrastive narrative perspective. In Ngugi's *A Grain of Wheat*, the "yesterday-today" perspective is supplemented by the "today-tomorrow" perspective. The very presentation of the novel stresses this important double perspective of analepsis and prolepsis. For example, Ngugi carefully uses quotations placed at the very beginning of his books to stress his central ideas. If the critics have ignored this signpost, it remains nonetheless graphically visible. The existence, side by side, of the two perspectives is significant for the general direction of the narrative. They are presented, face to face, on the first pages of the book through a note and a quotation from the Bible. The two passages are not accidentally juxtaposed. A careful scrutiny of the pieces yields access to the heart of the problem delineated by the novel. The first passage emphasizes the "yesterday-today" perspective, the second embraces the uncertainty about the outcome of the struggle. Together, they produce a chronicle of the African quest for land and freedom. They also impose a contrastive perspective of characters, places, and events on the reader.

The first passage lays an equal claim to history and fiction, while emphasizing the contemporary nature of the setting and the realism of the condition of the landless peasants. Although the product of imagination, *A Grain of Wheat* persuasively takes the form of a historical chronicle in order to create a myth of transformation toward eventual social justice. It combines the product of imagination and the teachings of the past in a well-woven narrative. This can be seen in the following quotation from Ngugi's note.

> Although set in Kenya, all the characters in this book are fictitious. Names like that of Jomo Kenyatta and Waiyaki are unavoidably mentioned as part of the history and institutions of our country. But the situation and the problems are real—sometimes too painfully real for the peasants who fought the British yet who now see all that they fought for being put on one side. (*Grain*, p. vi)

The second passage suggests the future through a natural phenomenon. By emphasizing the necessity for the grain to die in order to be reborn, the quotation does more than reassert the title of the book; it also suggests the dialectical nature of the relation between death and life. The quotation insists on the necessity of change as a fundamental law of nature and convincingly outlines the process of transformation in nature and in society.

While the first passage emphasizes the historical connection to the present, the second passage embodies the lessons from history and stresses a future perspective. The global perspective is formally exemplified by the use of flashbacks and the narration of the future plans and dreams of the characters.

Despite the difficult period it covers, *A Grain of Wheat* is a novel of hope. The hope that a grain of wheat is sown that will germinate to feed hungry souls is kept alive among the victims of the colonial rule. Rebirth and regeneration lie in front of despair and death. Govind Narain Sharma accurately analyzes this theme. I must, however, take exception to Sharma's statement that the novel marks "the end of brokenness and alienation and the restoration to wholeness and community."[1] On the contrary, the novel shows a divided community, remarkably partisan, and resolutely drawn to class distinction as well as class confrontations. Above all, the narrative deplores the fact that the peasant freedom fighters are the victims of political conditions. Although they signaled, and continue to signal, to the left, the politicians have, alas, made a turn to the right. In a sense, the novel demystifies the official Uhuru.[2]

A Grain of Wheat is about social transformation. It depicts a process of change from colonialism to Uhuru, through a revolutionary war, and the subsequent appropriation of the fruit of the Mau Mau war of liberation by the local African landlords. The land that is the major reason for the war is appropriated by the local politicians, as *Petals of Blood* reveals. Gikonyo registers the real quality of the transformation.

> The bus, called A DILIGENT CHILD, belonged to one of those people in Rung'ei whose fortunes were made during the war for independence. Those were men who through active cooperation with the colonial government had acquired trade licences and even loans to develop their business. Although Gikonyo was hopeful, he was slightly bitter about having to go all the way to Nairobi. Few M.P.s had offices in their constituencies. As soon as they were elected, they ran to Nairobi and were rarely seen in their areas, except when they came back with other national leaders to address big political rallies. (*Grain*, p. 71)

Petals of Blood continues *A Grain of Wheat*. It perpetuates the saga of the "tree of life" as prophesied by Mugo wa Kibiro. The scene is Kenya, but the range of the concerns is, of course, broader. The memory of the Mau Mau revolution shares the thematic center of the novel with the land issue (a theme already present in *Weep Not, Child*), the feminist cause, industrialization, the emergence of a class of workers, and the social struggles between them and the national bourgeoisie.

Ngugi's writing constantly displays a commitment to these themes. Indeed, their presence in all his works ties them together. *Petals of Blood* continues and expands on the theme that was central to the project of *A Grain of Wheat*, as is apparent to young Karega.

> The people I knew, the people I had seen creating new worlds, are hazy images in my memory: *and the seed we planted together with so much faith, hope, blood and tears: where is it now?* I ask

myself: where is the new force, *what's the new force that will make the seed sprout and flower?* (*Petals*, p. 46; my emphasis)

The Metaphor

Petals of Blood is a highly symbolic novel. But the most illuminating metaphor in the book is the flower, "petals of blood." It starts the novel, provides its title, and closes the narrative. Whereas the children name it, its description is provided by Munira, who in his prison cell, should now know of his own farsightedness or vision. In effect, Munira is the arsonist who burnt three businessmen in a house. Of the characters involved in the story, Munira was, at the onset, the least likely to take an action with such devastating political significance. But throughout the novel, his vision is stained with blood. It is a vision of "violence of thought, violence of sight, violence of memory." He acknowledges his apprehension of the metaphor, but it is only from the "arrogant confidence of hindsight."

Blood, violence, and power are three elements that define the character of the novel. *Petals of Blood* is a story about power struggle, displayed in the confrontations between the individual characters and the class conflicts within the society. It is a novel about violence, with sexual violence presiding over much of the novel. Blood becomes only an aspect of social violence.

The violence that Munira sees is a dehumanizing phenomenon that attacks thinking, vision, and memory. Powerlessness in itself becomes a form of violence. Munira is hurt by the realization of his powerlessness to save Karega. He confirms the validity of the metaphor at the end of the novel. The entire novel is underlined by this overriding metaphor. It combines the three elements of power (also believed to be the quest of Wanja), violence, and blood to form a narrative network with finely depicted interactions. The three elements are outlined by Munira at the beginning of the novel, but the reader has little reason to believe in the validity of his social analysis implicitly offered as the cause for spilling blood. Indeed, the reader has very little reason to believe the suspect instead of relying on the ability of the strange Inspector Godfrey to unravel the mystery.

The society in which the crime occurred is stricken by the same disease that struck the red flower, the petals of blood. Munira is the one who diagnoses the disease by noticing three of its symptoms: (1) it was eaten by a worm; (2) it cannot bear fruit; and (3) flowers do not need worms—they need light. Similarly, the society is an infertile society, eaten in the center by hidden parasites. Ngugi's skill consists in suspending the two interpretations of the significance of Munira's arrest. Inspector Godfrey is investigating a crime; he wants the criminal. But from his prison cell, Munira perceives a different criminal. He believes society itself is responsible for the murder. The narrator then plunges in the heart of the story.

The following passage offers a key to understanding the novel, as it puts Munira in the position of a reflective man. The passage also underscores the violence of the men against the women and the struggle of the women for power (an important theme of the novel).

> But how can I, a mortal, help my heart's fluttering . . ., I who knew Abdulla, Nyakinyua, Wanja, Karega? Have I not leafed through the heart of each? In all our conversations and schemes and remembrances of the past . . . was always struck by the razor-blade tension at the edges of our words. Violence of thought, violence of sight, violence of memory. I can see that now. In this prison twilight certain things, groves, hills, valleys, are sharper in outline even though set against a sight. There was a time I used to think that I was saving him, might have saved her and Abdulla too. Then I suddenly saw Karega about to tumble headlong down the path I myself had gingerly trodden and I was struck by my lack of power to hold him back, though I wanted to. For one week I would picture Wanja laughing at our frail efforts to extricate ourselves from her vast dreams and visions; for I now knew . . . that all she wanted was power, power especially over men's souls . . . to avenge herself of the evil done to her in the past. (*Petals*, p. 45)

As can be seen from this excerpt, Munira is mainly concerned with moral issues. In his view, immorality, greed, and selfishness are the causes of the woes that befall Ilmorog. His obsession with moral issues triggers in him the very violence he spoke against. When the novel opens, Munira is held in custody by the police as a suspect in the case of arson that left several people dead. From then on, the narrative becomes a long flashback, ostensibly unraveling Inspector Godfrey's investigation. This approach justifies the multiplicity of narrative perspectives and voices in the novel as the Inspector gathers different testimonies, including Munira's elaborate one. His testimony is really a soul-searching investigation, carefully written in prison, as if it were intended for posterity; however, its aim is not to find the arsonist, but to explain the reason or reasons behind crime itself. Thus, *Petals of Blood*, like *Perpetua*, is also a detective story; but it unravels the transformation of a village and its inhabitants through the testimonies of two different, yet complementary, characters.

Petals of Blood: A Detective Story

Petals of Blood is a detective story, depicting the investigation of a murder. Inspector Godfrey, a criminal investigation expert, arrives in Ilmorog to work on the case. He is a respectful person, calm and enlightened. When Inspector Godfrey authorized Munira to write a statement, he could not have made the prisoner happier. This event forms the narrative junction of the story. In his conclusion, Munira diametrically opposes the findings of the detective. Yet both "detectives" investigated the same crime. Inspector Godfrey's inquiry is the investigation of a murder; for him, the crime is another jigsaw puzzle to unravel. Munira's conclusion is moral, but Godfrey's is technical. These two investigations are the occasion for the narrator to give us a complete history of the case, enriched by a great variety of points of view and characters, witnesses and actors alike. Of all the suspects, Munira is the only one who, with his moral conclusion, really disorients the otherwise stern Inspector Godfrey.

Petals of Blood is divided into four parts; each part is subtitled and bears quotations from the Song of Solomon, William Blake, Walt Whitman, Amilcar Cabral, and the Bible. The book itself owes its title to a poem from *The Swamp*, by the Caribbean poet Derek Walcot.

Part one of the novel is titled "Walking." It describes the Ilmorog encounter of the major protagonists. They have come to Ilmorog for some personal and obscure reasons. When Munira arrives in Ilmorog, Abdulla, a former Mau Mau freedom fighter, is already an established storekeeper. Wanja has returned to live with her grandmother; she hopes to be blessed with a child. Munira is "in flight from the challenges of his own life," like his unsuccessful marriage. Karega, son of a squatter, has been expelled from the prestigious Siriana High School for taking part in a student protest. But so far, the reader knows very little of the past of these characters and the goals they aim to achieve. Unsatisfied with the lack of opportunities in the village, Wanja and Karega go to the Highlands, but Limuru has little to offer them. They meet Munira and all three return to the drought-stricken Ilmorog. They form a delegation and set out on the road to Nairobi to seek help from the political representative of their administrative region.

The second part of the novel is subtitled "Toward Bethlehem," in search of the savior. According to Gerald Moore, this part of the story is

> deliberately invested with an epic atmosphere. Abdulla now emerges as a figure of valour and skill, the reincarnation of Kenya's ancient warriors, whilst Nyakinyua becomes the bard and storyteller of the group. The events of the journey to the city take on a fabulous character even while they occur and soon afterwards retreat into legend; they become part of Ilmorog's heroic tradition.[3]

Their adventures in the city are eye-opening for the destitute peasants of Ilmorog. The urban-based politicians once again turn their backs on their needy rural constituency. The delegation returns to its dry lands and hungry families.

In part three, "To Be Born," the rains finally fall, miraculously returning the village to its ordinary, self-sustaining life. There is even the revival of Theng'eta beer-making, which had been declared illegal by the colonial government. A love affair between Karega and Wanja soon sparks the bitter jealousy of the schoolmaster. Karega leaves Ilmorog, and a plane crash kills Abdulla's "other leg," his faithful donkey. Gradually, powerful people from Nairobi move into Ilmorog, swiftly crawling into its intimate life and rapidly acquiring land.

> Dancing groups formed; drinking parties came over: Ilmorog had overnight become famous well beyond the only shepherds and aged peasants who roamed and sang to the soil and to the elephant grass, looking to the sky for sun and rain. (*Petals*, p. 258)

But the new festive atmosphere does not presage happier days for Ilmorog. After all, it is the airplane of the invading powerful businessmen that kills the famous donkey that belonged to Abdulla, the former Mau Mau fighter. The new businessmen arrive into Ilmorog with a disaster, and they disrupt the quiet life of the village. They expropriate the peasants by luring them into taking loans that they are unable to repay, and they eliminate the small entrepreneur by taking away Wanja's brewing rights. Part four, subtitled "La Luta Continua," describes the subversive influence of outside power brutally imposed on Ilmorog.

> By this time, Inspector Godfrey has gathered enough pieces of information to solve his jigsaw puzzle.
> This case interested him immediately, especially because of the types of personalities it had brought together. Chui—educationist and businessman; Hawkins Kimeria—a business tycoon; Abdulla—a petty trader; Karega—a trade unionist; Mzigo—a teacher educationist turned businessman: Munira—a teacher and man of God; Wanja—a prostitute. And all this in what was basically a New Town. He wondered how many other people it would bring together. (*Petals*, p. 44)

Anyone of the four people (Abdulla, Munira, Wanja, and Karega) could be the criminal. The conviction of Munira—a man of God from a well-to-do family—is unsettling even for the detective. For if Karega, the militant trade unionist from a squatter family, had committed the crime, it would have been easy to link its motives to his political activities. But for Munira to commit a murder of the influential businessmen on the basis of safeguarding morality smacks of fanaticism. Inspector Godfrey nails down the scholarly investigator of Ilmorog when he finally asks,

> "Mr. Munira . . . what were you doing in Ilmorog Hill on the Sunday morning after the arson?" Munira looked at the officer. He read everything in his eyes.
> "So you know?" he asked quietly.
> "Yes, Mr. Munira . . . the rulers of every world have their laws, their policemen, and their judges and . . . the law's executioners . . . not so? I am afraid, Mr. Munira, that I am only a policeman of this world. And I'll now formally charge you with burning Wanja's house and causing the deaths of three men." (*Petals*, pp. 331-32)

It is unsettling to witness crimes triggered by religious conflicts in the society. Yet it is less the crime itself that disturbs the inspector than the history of Munira. This is indicated by the interrogation and subsequent narratives of Munira's relationship with his wealthy father. Munira has resolved to curse his father's exploitation of other people and his failure to be faithful to the Christian laws he taught his children to abide by. Munira refuses to live in the shadow of his father's business. He forsakes his father's wealth and life-style, and identifies with the life of a small community of poor peasants, workers, and prostitutes. For twelve years, he shares their struggles and participates in their dreams. Munira's action becomes a devastating condemnation of the elite class in which he was born and raised. In spite of himself, his final action is charged with political connotations. If it had been committed by the other suspects, the crime would have been interpreted differently by officials like Inspector Godfrey. If Karega had committed the murder, it would have appeared as a political crime by a "communist." If Wanja had committed the crime, it would have been recorded as a simple act of vengeance from a prostitute. If Abdulla were the arsonist, the murder would have been perceived as the angry response from a petty trader who once belonged to Mau Mau. What could be Munira's reason or reasons? It is hard for the inspector to explain them, although he knows them intuitively.

Munira's rejection of his father's life-style, and thus his social class, is the main source of his long period of alienation from all social groups beyond the classes he teaches.[4] This situation continues until Wanja helps pull him into the heart of the Ilmorog community. Finally, he identifies with the life and goals of his chosen community. He seems more dangerous than the other suspects because of what Inspector Godfrey sees as his unpredictability and his "betrayal" of his native class:

> it was people like Munira who really disturbed him. How could Munira have repudiated his father's immense property? Could property, wealth, status, religion, plus education not hold a family together? Inspector Godfrey decided that it was religious fanaticism! Yet from his own experience in the police force, such fanaticism was normally found among the poor. Human beings: they could never be satisfied! (*Petals*, p. 334)

It is true that the two murder investigations carried out by Inspector Godfrey and schoolmaster Munira do not coincide in their conclusions. Munira demands divine justice, and Inspector Godfrey has faith in social laws and earthly justice. He refuses to search any further, admitting his mercenary role in society.

Inspector Godfrey is extremely class-conscious. As long as social classes stay in their places, he finds it almost a pleasure to unravel crime puzzles. But the emergence of the hybrid social creature that Munira represents is unsettling to him. Those people who move from a rich class into a poor class, not by accident but by moral preference, appear unusual and strange. The motive behind this denial of riches and material comfort in favor of moral satisfaction eludes the inspector. But Munira's action brings the issue of class distinction into clear focus in the narrative. Munira is not the only character in the novel who experienced social mobility—Inspector Godfrey himself is an example of the classic upward mobility success—but he certainly is the only one who willingly experiences it in reverse.

In the end, the novel is the story of two diametrically opposed worldviews: a materialist perspective represented by Inspector Godfrey, the businessmen, and the politicians; and a moral perspective represented by Munira, and the peasants and workers of Ilmorog. The novel focuses on the power struggle between the social classes, a theme that Ngugi sketches in *Weep Not, Child* and develops in *A Grain of Wheat*. It marks the violent birth of a class society during the country's quest for land, justice, and peace.[5] The power is still in the hands of those people who Gikonyo, in the previous novel, castigated, even as he erroneously saw Mugo as some kind of a heroic figure.

> It is people like you who ought to have been the first to taste the fruits of independence. But now, whom do we see riding in long cars and changing them daily as if motor cars were clothes? It is those who did not take part in the movement, the same who ran to the shelter of schools and universities and administration. At political meetings you hear them shout: Uhuru, Uhuru, we fought for. Fought where? (*Petals*, p. 80)

The murder that Munira is charged with appears as his only way of exercising power over men who were otherwise completely out of his reach. But his own view is of the mystical kind. He does not condone political struggles; he condones righteousness. The liberation he seeks is simply individualist and religious. He believes that he has rendered the city cleaner by chasing the evils of prostitution and big money away. It is Inspector Godfrey, the conscientious guardian of the ruling elite, who truly realizes the class nature of Munira's dissatisfaction with society. The inspector summarily dismisses the matter as another example of human fanaticism and inability to find satisfaction. By so doing, he hopes to exorcise the evil spirit from the son who rejects his father, or in other words, his social class.

Notes 4

[1] This thesis emerges, albeit in different ways, in the following critical studies: Govind Narain Sharma, "Ngugi's Christian Vision: Theme and Pattern in *A Grain of Wheat*," *African Literature Today*, no. 10 (1979): 167-76; Ime Ikkideh, "Ngugi wa Thiong'o: The Novelist as Historian," in *A Celebration of Black and African Writing*, ed. Bruce King and Kolowale Ogungbesan (London: Oxford University Press; Zaria: Ahmadou Bello University Press, 1975), 204-16; Leslie Monkman, "Kenya and the New Jerusalem in *A Grain of Wheat*," *African Literature Today*, no. 7 (1975): 111-16; Peter Nazareth, "Is *A Grain of Wheat* a Socialist Novel?" in *Literature and Society in Modern Africa* (Nairobi: East African Literature Bureau, 1972), 128-54; Edgar Wright, ed., *The Critical Evaluation of African Literature* (London: Heinemann, 1973); and Eustace Palmer, *The Growth of African Literature*, (London: Heinemann, 1980).

[2] For a discussion of the significance of Uhuru in the novels of Ngugi, see Christ Wanjala, *For Home and Freedom* (Nairobi: Kenya Literature Bureau, 1980), and Lewis Nkosi, *Tasks and Masks: Themes and Styles of African Literature* (London: Longman, 1981).

[3] Gerald Moore, *Twelve African Writers* (Bloomington: Indiana University Press, 1980), 284.

[4] For an appraisal of the theme of class struggles in *Petals of Blood*, see Ntongela Masilela, "Ngugi wa Thiong'o's *Petals of Blood*," *Ufahamu* 9, no. 2 (1979): 9-28.

[5] While he discusses Ngugi's depiction of class conflicts in the novel, Bernth Lindfors correctly underlines the mythopoeic vein of the narrative: "Like all successful popular literature, *Petals of Blood* has great mythopoeic power. It presents ideas and images which are invested with a compelling logic of their own, forcing us imaginatively to transcend everyday realities. The process of reading such works enables us to see a portion of the world anew and thus to revaluate our complacent assumptions about what is and what should be. This hallucinatory experience can yield great psychological satisfaction, awakening in us an impulse to dream more boldly, unconstrained by mundane facts." Bernth Lindfors, *"Petals of Blood* as a Popular Novel" (Paper presented at the African Literature Association Annual Conference, Clairemont, Calif., April 1981), 7.

5

Stylization in the Ruben and Mau Mau Trilogies

This chapter explores the narrative styles that characterize the Ruben trilogy by Mongo Beti and the Mau Mau trilogy by Ngugi wa Thiong'o. It considers stylistic elements that are common to the trilogies (e.g., the utilization of a collective narrator) and examines their relationship to another form, namely oral literature. The trilogies incorporate elements of oral literature, such as songs, praise names, and the initiatory journey. Taken together, this borrowing reveals the writers' stylization. In his study of "Literary Indebtedness," J. T. Shaw defines stylization as a work "in which an author suggests for an artistic purpose another author or literary work, or even the style of an entire period, by a combination of style and materials."[1] The artistic scene in Africa is conducive to written literatures borrowing from the oral literatures because of the contiguous developments of the two forms as well as the dominant stature of oral literature. Indeed, it is the popular literary expression on the African continent.

Although heroic narratives such as *Sundiata*, *The Mwindo Epic*, or *Moneblum* as told today share the same geographic scene as *Remember Ruben* and *A Grain of Wheat*, they reflect different periods. Beti and Ngugi base their stylization on the oral narrative and, more precisely, the epic narrative.

The Collective Narrator

The use of a collective narrator in the novels by Beti and Ngugi is an innovation in the context of contemporary African literature. It inevitably raises questions about the purpose of the "we" narrator, whose version of the events that compose the stories carries so much weight. One wonders about the identity of the narrator and about the artistic role that is thus aimed at.

In a very engaging essay on *Remember Ruben*, Eloise A. Brière makes an important contribution toward the definition of the collective narrator of the Ruben novels.[2] The critic defines the "nous" ("we," collective narrator) as the citizens of Ekoundoum who are involved in a collective cleansing ritual, a cathartic project that necessitates the elicitation of past events; this cathartic project is carried out by a narrator who is also the subject of the narrative.

The collective narrator enjoys a new identity. This identity emerges as a result of the transformations brought about by the struggle for the liberation of Ekoundoum. The freedom and unity that are attained strengthen the narrative of the transformational process. The so-called collective voice often includes several distinct individuals. Brière argues that the presence of multiple voices guarantees the credibility of the narrative.

Due to the presence of multiple points of view, one could doubt the validity of the collective narrator. Since voices other than the "nous" are included as individual contributions to the narrative, it may seem more appropriate to speculate about the collective narrator as a group of narrators with individual voices that, at times, are in total disagreement with one another about the significance of certain events. On closer look, it appears that the so-called narrators are not extensions of the collective voice because they are different individuals who often speak for themselves (Evariste and Mor-Kinda, for example). Neither are they surrogates, since the functions they fulfill are different. These secondary narrators do not lose their individual identities.

The unity of the collective narrator is insured by its central position in the story, giving the narrative direction, and choosing which other narrative contributions to retain or dismiss. The collective narrator selects and rearranges the factors that transform Ekoundoum; thus, it brings order where chaos had been rampant and makes the past intelligible to the present audience. Furthermore, the narrator's talent in providing a convincing synthesis of past events validates its reliability to the reader. Thus, the multiplicity of narrative voices reaffirms the power and authority of the collective narrator.

The discrepancy of tones displayed in the story is linked with the absence of the narrator from places where certain events occurred or the lack of reliable eyewitness reports. In this regard, the degree of uncertainty on the part of the narrator is proportionally equal to the distance that separates it from the places where the narrated events occur. The episodes of the narrative that take place outside of Ekoundoum, particularly in Kola-Kola and Fort-Nègre, are more doubtful in their details than the episodes that deal directly with Ekoundoum.

Beti uses the collective narrator in two of his novels, and Ngugi gradually employs the "we" narrator in the Mau Mau trilogy. According to Florence Stratton, the basic point of view in Ngugi's novels is the third person, but there is also at least one other narrator speaking from inside the events and who represents the expression of a collective consciousness. This inside voice is represented by the marker "you" in *The River Between* and *Weep Not, Child*. In *A Grain of Wheat*, the marker is used in part one, and in the rest of the novel, it is combined with "we." The latter marker becomes more and more prominent—though not exclusive—throughout *Petals of Blood*. Why does Ngugi gradually drop the exclusive use of "you" to adopt the marker "we" in subsequent narratives?

Stratton defines the "you" of *The River Between* and *Weep Not, Child*:

> the indefinite or generic "you" meaning "people in general." It is only personal by style, not as a result of inherent meaning, and thus, although it has the effect of involving the reader in events the bond between speaker and reader is comparatively weak. Also although its use denotes a speaker who is inside the events, it does not refer to the participants in a speech event itself. In other words, there is no first person narrator, but rather a consciousness through which the experiences of the people are filtered.[3]

Whereas the marker "you" is generic in the first novel, the "we" and "you" of the subsequent novels are personal pronouns; "we" refers to the internal narrative voice of the events and other participants, and the "you" refers to the reader as addressee.

This dual style offers the advantages of the first person narration and seeks to appeal more directly to the emotional involvement of the reader. The method is an attempt on the part of the novelist to make up for the privileged closeness that exists between the oral narrator and his audience, which is ordinarily lacking between the writer and his readers. In this insightful study, Stratton shows Ngugi's masterful use of markers to convey the feeling that the reader is "participating" in a collective experience.

In the Mau Mau trilogy, the narrative also incorporates secondary narrative voices. In *A Grain of Wheat* and *Petals of Blood*, the "we" indicates the presence of the general narrative voice that encompasses all other individual narrative contributions. But the secondary narrators remain important in both novels. In *A Grain of Wheat*, Mumbi recalls the Emergency to Mugo, and Gikonyo narrates the ordeal of the detention camp. In *Petals of Blood*, Wanja tells Abdulla the story of her seduction, and Abdula tells his experiences as a Mau Mau freedom fighter. These passages of narratives within the narrative are indicated by an opening statement that breaks the constant use of "we," substituting a personal individual voice to the collective narrator's voice. Finally, the secondary narratives play the role of case histories that record the painful experiences of the individual characters. These case histories document the transformations.

The same quality appears in the Ruben trilogy, as evidenced by the discussion that opens the second part of *Lament*. The protagonists of the main events that took place in Ekoundoum are engaged in a discussion, and Evariste's disagreement with Mor-Kinda's analysis of the events is reported twice: "Speak for yourself, Commander," and further on, "Hold on a minute please, Commander. Speak for yourself" (*Lament*, p. 108). Although they agree on the main significance of the events, the leaders of the liberation of Ekoundoum disagree on details.

Their continuous disagreement on the quality of their approach for liberating Ekoundoum is overshadowed by the more authoritative voice of the collective narrator. Its voice presents itself as a more factual, clear-sighted, and encompassing narrator. As soon as it takes over the narration of the events, the reader forgets the disagreement of the Rubenists, to turn to the more reliable collective narrator:

> The fact is that, for anyone capable of encompassing with a single glance the various turns of fortune in their campaign against the chief and his allies, everything happened as if our Kola-Kolans had indeed been defeated at the beginning, before they could even engage in battle, as frequently occurs in projects undertaken in the expectation of an easy victory that can be achieved almost without striking a blow. (*Lament*, p. 108)

As can be seen from this quotation Beti, like Ngugi, grants a lot of authority to the collective narrator. The power of its vision embodies the consciousness of a collective quest for freedom, which is qualified by a historical dimension. Stratton's essay on Ngugi's narrative style stresses the popular nature of the collective narrator of the Mau Mau trilogy.

> Through making the people a character in his novels, Ngugi not only achieves a very strong statement of theme, but, particularly in the novels, appeals to the reader so effectively that the reader eventually feels that the voice of the people embraces his own.[4]

Although this conclusion refers to *A Grain of Wheat*, the critic finds the entire novel "flawed in a minor way by the unaccountable switch in pronouns partway through."[5] Stratton's essay would have gained by mentioning that the entire narrative of *A Grain of Wheat* rests on the suspense generated by the news of a secret investigation undertaken by the freedom fighters. The investigation involves a case of treason that culminated in the capture and hanging of Kihika, who was the local leader of the Mau Mau freedom fighters. The suspense is heightened by the coming Uhuru celebration, when the outcome of the investigation is expected to become public. In that regard, the beginning of the narrative is rather slow, generally panoramic, and somewhat impersonal, as the narrator/investigator gropes around among the survivors, feeling "the smoldering battlefield" of Thabai. It is hardly surprising that this part of the narrative should be dominated by the use of the indefinite pronoun "you" in its meaning of "people in general." As the narrative advances toward the day of Uhuru celebration, the stakes appear particularly significant for individuals like Karanja, who become prime suspects since they fought the war on the side of the Homeguards. Few people in the community seem to look forward to a public trial on the very day of Uhuru celebration, marking the end of a long and cruel war. At this point, the narrative is heightened as it acquires tempo and becomes more personal and upbeat. Again, it is hardly surprising that Ngugi shifts to personal pronouns. On the contrary, his dexterous manipulation of the pronouns is further evidence of his acute and sophisticated sense of skillful composition.

Elements of Oral Literature in the Trilogies

In discussing the place and role of the collective narrator, this study indicates the writers' attempt to draw from the qualities of the communal experience in order to render the atmosphere of transformations that affect the communities. The distance the writers adopt in regard to the traditional novel by listening to a narrator representing the majority of the oppressed people struggling toward their collective betterment is a reflection of the artists' attempt at stylizing after heroic narratives. The use of the collective narrator as a translator of communal aspirations and changes is only one of several stylistic innovations made by Beti and Ngugi. The innovations include the use of the initiatory journey to propel the story forward, the use of popular songs and fables to characterize situations as well as individuals, the creation of heroic characters with a highly symbolic dimension, and the use of praise names.

The Initiatory Journey

Since the novel always involves a quest, it would seem that the presence of a quest in the Mau Mau trilogy and the Ruben trilogy simply responds to a formal requirement. In addition to this formal feature, however, both trilogies incorporate an initiatory journey that molds the personality of the subject through a series of challenging encounters and experiences. When the journey ends, the subject discovers a new self and bears a new identity.

Although this narrative feature is not exclusively African, it is a consistent element of the oral narrative in Africa, which is subsequently extended into, and adapted to, the novel. In the wider cultural context, young men and women are traditionally initiated into adult society through a ceremony that unfolds in three phases: the separation of the neophyte from the original community, the transitional period, and the process of reintegration.

The definition of initiation offered by Aliko Songolo is most helpful in that it includes the utilization of the ceremonial structure in artistic creations.[6] But in order to apply this definition to the trilogies, it is necessary to modify the terms of the phases while maintaining the order in which they proceed. For in the trilogies, the second phase of the initiatory journey is best described as a period of exile, since the subject is unaware of its transitional quality. This is despite the fact that the phase reenacts the prophecy of Mugo wa Kibiro in the Mau Mau trilogy and the prophecy of the old man of Ekoundoum in the Ruben trilogy. Furthermore, the subject unconsciously stresses the myths of the return and restitution of the Gikuyu and the Essazam. The idea of a transition presupposes that as the subject sets out on its journey it is conscious of performing a part of the teleological movement of the Creator. But Mor-Zamba does not even foresee the reasons of his tribulations in Kola-Kola and Fort-Nègre. Similarly, Munira hardly envisioned such a momentous event as he ended up participating in during his stay in Ilmorog. The characters do not know that they are undergoing an initiatory journey, and the citizens of Ekoundoum and Ilmorog are unaware of future developments. Only the collective narrator in both trilogies can, and does, speak in terms of transition, since the stories are told in retrospect. As for the idea of reintegration into the original community, it might suggest that the communities remained stable, unchanged, and frozen during the exile of the hero. This understanding of reintegration would be inappropriate for our study simply because the communities undergo profound changes. It is safer to speak of the return of the hero. Finally, separation is an adequate description of the first phase of the initiatory journey for this study because, even at the collective level, there is at least one partition of the subject, as manifested by the divisions that split the citizens of Ekoundoum, Thabai, and Ilmorog into conflicting groups. As a consequence of this kind of emotional, material, and ideological partition of the peoples, the cities bear the signs of a separation, a parting with their traditional order, to acquire new social structures and relations by the end of the initiatory process.

Like the collective journey, the individual initiatory journey involves a painful metamorphosis. Whether collective or individual, the initiatory journey implies a transformation of the neophyte that may or may not be publicly sanctioned. For example, Mor-Zamba is tacitly recognized as the new leader of Ekoundoum, and Karega is seen by the workers of Ilmorog as their leader.

The use of this initiatory structure as an archetype in the narratives is an artistic device that allows the narrator to chronicle the transformation of the neophyte, to give purpose and credibility to the undertaking, and, in the case of the trilogies, to justify the myths of transformation as well as verify the prophecies. The journey is made even more credible in the trilogies since the subject is unconscious of the fact that it is reenacting the myths.

Songs, Tales, Praise Names and Their Function in the Narratives

In general, it can be stated that an epic performance includes parts that are sung and parts that are spoken as straight narrative. In his introduction to *The Ozidi Saga*, J. P. Clark remarks,

> While action at such stages is described as well as demonstrated, it
> is the responsibility of the story-teller to conjure up by word the
> beauty and pity pregnant in the situation.[7]

This general pattern of song mode and narrative (unsung) mode is found in
all the epic stories mentioned in this study. Although there are no songs in
the Ruben trilogy, the reader finds numerous songs in the Mau Mau trilogy.
In *A Grain of Wheat*, some are popular songs of the Mau Mau freedom
fighters; some songs appear in English translation, whereas others are
presented in Gikuyu; certain songs describe the condition of the oppressed
in forced labor, others celebrate the memory of people like Wambuku or
Mugo, who distinguished themselves as heroes during the struggle (pp. 26,
92, 123, 164, 204). In *Petals of Blood*, there are songs of African unity,
church songs, blues songs, love songs, and work songs (pp. 263, 165,
264, 288, 338).

The songs in *Sundiata* and in the Mau Mau trilogy pinpoint the high
moments of the narratives to emphasize a sentiment (anger, love, or fear) or
a quality in a character. Though there are no songs in the Ruben trilogy, the
reader finds fables, all of which are narrated by Mor-Kinda to illustrate
future plans or present situations. In *Lament*, there are five such fables.
There are four fables in part one of the novel, and part three announces the
shift of the narrative to the description of the role of women through the
fifth fable. This original narrative device offers several advantages. It
shows that beneath the apparent disorder in which the Rubenists seem
caught, there is a serious method of conducting a war of liberation. It is a
method that combines theory and practice. The occasional discrepancies
between theory and practice do not altogether invalidate the method. The
fifth fable, in which the participation of the women in the liberation effort is
given as indispensable for its success, is subsequently proven to be the
valid approach. These fables are reminiscent of the short didactic tales that
are abundantly used in Africa and that constitute an element as important as
the proverb in the African approach to discourse.

In addition to the fables, Beti uses praise names to describe characters,
as is often done in orature.[8] For example, Mor-Kinda is called "Jo the
Juggler," a resourceful and intriguing man; Evariste, the youngest Rubenist,
is called "Sapak"; and Mor-Zamba is either called "Bumpkin" by his
irreverent friends or, more often, "The Lion Of Kola-Kola" or "The
Wandering Child" by the narrator.

Mongo Beti and the *Mbomo-mvet:* A Literary Kinship

In an interview with Anthony Biakolo, Beti mentions his indebtedness
to Chinua Achebe. After reading Achebe's *Things Fall Apart*, he realized

that stylistic features of oral narratives can become an enriching source in the hands of a skillful writer. His use of language, proverbs, and fables gives vigor and sweetness to the novels, and although the inspiration for epic illusion in his trilogy is probably not African in any exclusive sense, it is possible to show its specific closeness to the *mvet* tradition. Considered in its complete evolution, the trilogy suggests a kinship between the writer and the *mbomo-mvet* (the bard who tells *mvet* epic stories). Beti's novels are informed by an acute awareness of the Camerounian social, political, and cultural situation, and as discussed below, Beti's Ruben cycle is indebted to the *mvet* epic. Two well known texts—*Moneblum*, by Eno S. Belinga (Cameroun), and *Le Mvett*, by Tsira Ndong Ndoutoume (Gabon)—will serve as examples of *mvet* narrative.[9]

The *mvet* is an art form of the Bulu, Fang, and Beti peoples of Cameroun, Gabon, and Equatorial Guinea. According to Belinga, the word *mvet* designates three things: (1) a stringed instrument to which three calabashes are attached; (2) an epic song that is accompanied by this musical instrument; and (3) a literary genre in which epic literature, music, and traditional choreography are associated. The *mvet* is, at once, a recitation, a song, and a dance performed with a participating audience by the master *mvet* performer called *mbomo-mvet*.

According to scholars of orature, the *mvet* has a divine origin. It was revealed to the master artist Oyono Ada Ngono during a long initiation process. Oyono Ada Ngono was initiated into the art in the Upper Nile region. He is said to have received the following revelation: Jap-The Sun, Love, *Mvet* music, and Beauty; he was also taught that Love and Beauty are sisters. He received the teachings through three means: songs, creation myths, and anomastics. Belinga states that the *mvet* narrative combines the diverse elements of theogony, cosmogony, psychology, and physics that constitute the essential initiatory tradition shared by all the *mvet* poets of the same school. These elements are known as the Mysteries.

Beti's trilogy exhibits a close literary kinship with the epic *Mvett*. Although he has not cited a particular piece of oral narrative as a source, it is clear that he is familiar with the *mvet* tradition. According to Roger Mercier, Beti uses a stylistic feature from the *mvet* tradition in his novel *Mission terminée*.[10] He reveals that the use of plot summaries at the beginning of chapters in the novel are derived from an observation of *mvet* narrative techniques. Although many years have passed, it may be said that Beti has returned to the *mvet* as a literary source in his recent writing. There are striking resemblances in form, characterization, and theme between the *Moneblum* epic story and Beti's Ruben cycle.

Kinship of Form and Characterization

Structurally, the double itinerary of Mor-Zamba from Ekoundoum to Fort-Nègre and back is similar to the itinerary of Mekui-Mengomo, the hero of *Moneblum*. Mekui-Mengomo is exiled to the kingdom of the Moneblum, whence he returns to the kingdom of Akoma Mba, after a period of intense labor. There are similarities in the phases of the itinerary: Mor-Zamba experiences prison life in Camp Gouverneur Leclerc, and the hero of *Moneblum* is thrown in prison in the kingdom of the Moneblum.

Furthermore, both Mekui-Mengomo and Mor-Zamba go through many obstacles on their initiatory journeys as prisoners, and as active participants during their return journeys. It follows from this feature that the story gathers speed in the form of an action-packed saga.

The Ekan war heroes are found among the representatives of the Rock, the Iron, and the Hammer symbolism. It appears that Mor-Kinda, who finds all the war paraphernalia, is a Hammer character, i.e., the provider of tools; that Abena, who seeks a gun, is an Iron character; and that Mor-Zamba, who has a lot of strength and endurance, is a Rock character. Each of the three main characters in the Ruben cycle undoubtedly represents more than one element, but all three are war heroes as can be seen in the novels, and each one is distinguished from the others by his particular gift and ability.

If Mor-Zamba is likened to Akomo, Mekui-Mengomo is the direct descendent of Akomo. Both Mor-Zamba and Mekui-Mengomo show generosity and a sense of solidarity toward their fellow prisoners. Having taken the responsibility of leading them, Mekui-Mengomo tries to improve the conditions of the prisoners by liberating them from hard labor. Thus, alone, and by a few strokes of his sword, the hero builds two gigantic roads and cleans the entire kingdom of Efon-Ndon. Like Mor-Zamba, who became the tireless nurse of his fellow prisoners, Mekui-Mengomo takes care of the health of his companions. After work he gives them soap and clean clothes. They are both strong and brave characters.

In the epic narrative, the heroes are given praise names that describe their special aptitudes. Thus, Akomo is known as "The King Of Kings," "Knowledge," "The Immortal," "The Wise," "The Guide." In the trilogy, Mor-Kinda is known as "Jo The Juggler," "The Old Bad Boy Of Kola-Kola," "Commander," and "Messenger Of The Black Messiah"; Mor-Zamba is also called "The Lion Of Kola-Kola," "Defender Of The Weak," "The Terror Of The Saringala." Abena and Mor-Zamba share the name of "The Man Who Walks Carrying Thunder," and Ruben is known as "The Black Messiah."

Thematic Kinship

Exile is an important element of the narratives. Moneblum is exiled by his father, and Mor-Zamba is betrayed by the peers of his late grandfather; they "sold" him away to the colonial troops. The theme of the road that leads toward the unknown while opening new perspectives and creating new relationships is common to both narratives. Also, the theme of exile is accompanied by the introduction of prison in *Moneblum* and *Remember Ruben*. In both cases, the immediate cause of the exile is the character's quest for a spouse. Mekui-Mengomo is successful in his quest for a wife, whereas Mor-Zamba fails and subsequently turns away from this objective.

This contrast underlines an important thematic difference between the two narratives. For Beti, the gun, symbol of liberation, replaces the spouse in the story. This concern is verbalized by Abena, who is Mor-Zamba's brother in Akomo. After Mor-Zamba's failure to marry the daughter of Engamba, Abena goes on a quest for a gun. Despite this difference, Abena unconsciously repeats the odyssey of Mekui-Mengomo, albeit with a modified objective. Abena goes after the gun and brings it home to use it efficiently. Mekui-Mengomo brings home Nlem Okele Abum, from the kingdom of the Moneblum, as a spouse.

This transformation of the original myth is only one of many differences between these two narratives. By substitution, the writer transforms and adapts the myth to a new symbol. Thus, by making the myth espouse the breadth of our concerns, ambitions, and dreams, Beti not only places it in our time, but projects a vision of the future, the future of a liberated people. It is Mor-Kinda, the former houseboy of the colonial officer turned freedom fighter, who notices a similar vision in *Lament* (p. 88).

Although *Moneblum* is a good example of *mvet* narrative, it is neither the only one available in print nor necessarily the most representative. There is, of course, the quintessential reference volume, *Un Mvet de Zwe Nguema*,[11] collected, transcribed, translated, and annotated by Herbert Pepper and a team of scholars. (Zwe Nguema is described as the greatest *mbomo-mvet* alive in Gabon.) The book was published in the well-known series *Classiques africains*. The *Classiques africains* also has the most widely used style of bilingual presentation of oral narratives, preceded by a critical introduction and enriched with abundant notes. *Moneblum* fits very well this "scholarly model" of presentation.[12]

Yet, the same qualities of thorough, precise, and often stern presentation that have endeared the printed narratives to scholars of orature are also the very features that intimidate the larger public. As a consequence, the texts presented in the "popular model" are more widely distributed and better known among the reading public.

One of the finest *mvet* epics that successfully circumvents the hurdle of the scholarly presentation is simply, but significantly, titled *Le Mvett*. It was also written admittedly by a practitioner of *mvet* storytelling—in fact, an accomplished *mbomo-mvet*—and, judging by his book, an excellent writer as well. The author, Ndoutoume, whose contributions to making the epic by Zwe Nguema more accessible in print are acknowledged by the collector of *Un Mvet de Zwe Nguema*, spins his own epic rendition at a dizzying pace in the more than four hundred pages of the two volumes published by *Présence Africaine*.

According to Ndoutoume, the typical *mvet* epic narrates endless conflicts between the people of Oku (in the north) and the people of Engong (in the south). Whereas the people of Oku are the Mortals, Engong is the land of the powerful Immortals, who refuse to share the gift of immortality with their cousins of Oku.

Under ordinary circumstances, the people of Engong, though immortal, look and behave like the Mortals. However, in addition to their well-known immortality, they are all endowed with special powers of transformation. Therefore, they are seen by the Mortals as "men of power." Among them are giants, heroes, and sorcerers who marry daughters of the Mortals of Oku with whom they often have close family ties. The powers conferred upon the people of Engong by immortality constitute the essential difference between them and their less fortunate, but tenacious, cousins of Oku. Except for immortality, the people of Engong share all the strengths and weaknesses of the Mortals. This can be seen in the *mvet* characters introduced by Ndoutoume in his epic narrative.

Two of the highest ranking members of Engong are Akoma Mba The Dominant and his cousin Medza M'Otougou The Wealthy. It is said that both Akoma Mba and Medza M'Otougou received their special gifts on the same day from their uncle, the great sorcerer Nam Ndong. A man of two colors, black up to the waist and red from the waist up, Nam Ndong is said to have been the only witness of creation. During their visit, Nam Ndong presented to the young men a gift of two emblems to choose from. While Medza M'Otougou chose the emblem of material wealth, Okoma Mba surprised the sorcerer by selecting the emblem of power.[13]

Medza M'Otougou became the very symbol of wealth. His praise name is "The House Of A Wealthy Man Does Not Lack A Hero" for its protection. The most visible symbols of his wealth are his family, which forms a city of their own, and his farms, which are the largest anywhere north or south. He also owns innumerable cattle. Medza M'Otougou is a member of the Council of Elders in the land of the Immortals.

Akoma Mba is known as "The Supreme Chief" of the people of Engong, the man whose "Secret Has No Secrets," "Invincible Power," "Unlimited Creative Power." He is also known as the one who has shielded life from death and who can prolong or shorten life. He is both feared and envied by all; he is the very depth of knowledge, unique. But the people of Oku regard Akomo, "The Old Man Whose Age Is Unknown" as a very cruel being. He gained this reputation by murdering both his maternal cousin and his brother-in-law. Thus, Akomo, who is the judge of all disputes, is also guilty of willfully breaking two taboos.

Engouang Ondo, chief of the army of Engong, is known as "Favor And Violence," but also as "Peace And Goodness." He is said to be "beautiful like a palm tree" and is praised as

> the palm tree that protects the little growth, straight and hard like
> the pillar that supports the ceiling of the house. He sees by night,
> he sees by day, he sees the invisible.[14] (My translation)

The girls call him "The Magnificent." An example of the goodness of Engouang Ondo is given at the end of tome one of *Le Mvett*. Having finally disarmed and subdued the bold young chief Oveng Ndoumou Obame from Oku, whose pursuit of peace had led him to seek the total removal of metals (used for weapons) from the face of the earth, he proceeds to save his life, adopt him as a friend, and allow him to marry his sister.[15] It is this attitude of goodness toward their enemies that infuriates Ntoutoume Mfoulou, the founder of the Hammers and second in command to Engouang Ondo.

Ntoutoume Mfoulou, also known as "The Yes Of Mfoulou" because he said "yes" to death and "no" to life, lives off cruelty and killing. By the time he was born, all the other sons of Evine-Etsang had fathered children who became heroes and adopted emblems representing their special qualities. Mba Evine had begotten Akomo, who founded the emblem of the Rocks. Oyono Evine had many brave sons, who together created the emblem of the Iron, including the terrible Nze Medang and Angone Zok The Stutterer.

The family of the third son of Evine-Etsang was the only one without a hero and an emblem; therefore, it was the laughingstock of Engong. The birth of Ntoutoume Mfoulou put an end to the laughter. He appears to be even more cruel than Akomo Mba. He loves to fight, and he loves to destroy. He is happiest when there is a war. Ntoutoume Mfoulou created the emblem of "the Hammers that break rocks and soften iron." In addition to this terrifying emblem, he composed his own praise song to a tune he liked to whistle; the praise song is a challenge to death itself. Fast and impetuous, he is often compared to the python, and his father proudly calls him "The Volunteer For All Perilous Missions." He is the guardian of Engong, the land of the Immortals.

His favorite companion is Angone Zok Endong The Stutterer. They share the same passion for murder, tyranny, and pillage. When they are sent on a mission, Engouang Ondo must follow them and restrain the bloodthirsty duo. They obey his orders, but they do not like the chief of the army's calm, patient attitude toward the enemy and his undying passion for justice. Ntoutoume Mfoulou and Angone Zok Endong The Stutterer form a couple that complement each other. Whereas Ntoutoume Mfoulou is "The Hammer That Breaks Rocks And Softens Iron," Angone Zok Endong is known as "The Bellows That Soften Iron." Born of Medan Bore Endong, The Brave Of The Braves, and The Queen Of The Ghosts, Angone Zok Endong lives simultaneously in the world of the dead and the world of the living. For this reason, he is known as "The Fork" and as "The Dam That Stops The Flow Of Water And Mud And Controls The Course Of The Rivers." Angone can be expected in many places at once; so he is often likened to the squirrel that builds nine different nests during the rainy season. He sees everything. Angone Zok stutters, and when he is angry, he can only utter insults. Angone is feared throughout Oku, the land of the Mortals.

These terribly fearsome people of Engong, the Immortals, are the enemy of the people of Oku, who try to steal their secret of immortality. A hero is always created among the people of Oku to challenge the Immortals. All considered, the *mvet* sings of the great deeds of humans in their quest for immortality. Humans are the center of *mvet* literature and the Immortals are only a measure of the greatness of humans. They are at once the unfathomable depth of human intelligence and will, and the limit of human power. Therefore, the *mvet* sings of the greatness of humans, not of the gods. The principal theme of the *mvet* epic is human existence encoded between mortality and immortality.

Through its metaphorical language, the *mvet* teaches a philosophy of action. Ndoutoume insists that the *mvet* does not leave the realm of ordinary life. While revealing to us the internal, hidden side of life, it also teaches us about everyday existence.[16] However, action is always predicated on intelligence. *Mvet* characters who succeed in stealing the secret of immortality from Engong have done so not by using the strength of their muscles or invulnerability to fire and iron, but by taking an intelligent approach to the task. In tome one of *Le Mvett*, the young mortal Oveng Ndoumou Obame, having become a "man of power," goes to Engong in the quest for immortality. On the way, he falls in love with the beautiful Eyenga Nkabe, herself a woman of power. Unfortunately, he fights with, and breaks the leg of, her father. The old man demands revenge and sends his daughter to marry Engouang Ondo, chief of the army of Engong. The latter would then have no choice but to carry out his father-in-law's revenge. The old man's plan works, and the people of Engong attack the lonely mortal Oveng Ndoumou Obame. The young "man of power" decides to seek the heart of the immortal sister of Engouang Ondo, thus transforming his rivalry with the Immortals into an alliance and obtaining immortality.

A similar story is found in tome two of *Le Mvett*, when a Mortal, Elone Kam Afe, elopes with a daughter of Medza M'Otougou The Wealthy. Between these successful quests for immortality, the epic narrates several stories about "men of power" who insisted on a direct confrontation with the Immortals and were destroyed. It should be noted that in the *mvet* epic access to immortality depends on women. This is perhaps the reason why all *mvet* epic stories start with a man's heroic quest for a wife. It may also be the key to understanding the cryptic remark of Ndoutoume that "in the *mvet*, woman represents the secret that is not much talked about."[17]

The overriding philosophy that emerges from the *mvet* as a truly polyphonic genre is based on the permanence of intelligence, the emanation of divinity. If humans are encouraged to seek immortality through a philosophy of action guided by intelligence and the knowledge of the primacy of intelligence, it is because intelligence is the manifestation of God in humans. Intelligence is immortal. It is the supreme being, the origin of the will to act. This supreme being is the divine presence in humans. God is in ourselves. Humans, therefore, have the seeds of immortality. In order to find it, one must engage in a quest within oneself.

In the end, the *mvet* teaches a philosophy of action whose aim is self-improvement. Humans are destined to defeat death by seeking immortality. In the fantastic world of the *mvet*, infinite possibilities are suggested. Both the seeds of mortality and immortality are in the self, and it is incumbent upon humans to search within themselves and discover the seeds of immortality.[18] Life, therefore, is like the *mvet*, a struggle with oneself to enter inside of oneself in order to find the hidden realm of one's immortality. The initiates know that this represents human destiny, the ultimate destination of all great human deeds.

The expression of this quest is best realized through the metaphoric language of the *mbomo-mvet* and the philosophy of the *mvet* epic. The dance of the *mbomo-mvet*, his mime, his music, and the active participation of his audience constitute a reenactment of man's relentless internal struggle to attain the highest value embedded in himself, his immortality. The reenactment takes place in the universe itself, which in the metaphoric language of the *mvet* is a fantastic world, where time and space become inconsequential for the heroes and heroines who travel to Engong (the world of immortality, located in the south) and back to Oku (located north of Engong), where humans fly farther and higher than birds, where meetings are held on the moon, where water and fire are willed to rain on friends or foes, where rocks turn into deadly bombs, and where the bowels of the earth are transparent and easily penetrated. This is the fantastic par excellence.

At the same time, the reenactment of this Promethean undertaking of the Mortals in the *mvet* epic never entirely leaves the realm of the quotidian life. The Immortals come to Oku and play roles. These fearsome beings can be very amusing. At times, their behavior is ridiculous, and their thoughts ludicrous. They are often ridiculed, disoriented, and even humiliated by human intelligence.

Although it is impossible to isolate one *mvet* epic among the ones available in print as the principal source of inspiration for Beti's Ruben cycle, there is no doubt that the *mvet* as a genre played a critical role in the conception of these novels. Evidence of the similarity between the Ruben trilogy and the *mvet* is found in the predominance of action in Beti's novels as opposed to the philosophical or metaphysical inquiry in works such as C. A. Kane's *L'Aventure ambiguë*, Camara Laye's *Le regard du roi*, Ngal's *Giambatista Viko ou le viol du discours africain*, or Kofi Awoonor's *This Earth, My Brother*.[19] Instead of contemplative speculation, Beti's novels adhere to the philosophy of action for self-realization that is characteristic of the *mvet*.

Besides this similarity, there is the continuous tension between Mor-Zamba, the compassionate leader of the Rubenists, and his companions Jo The Juggler and Evariste that is reminiscent of the situation in *Le Mvett* between Engouang Ondo, chief of the army of Engong, and Ntoutoume Mfoulou and Angone Zok, his cruel lieutenants. The same tension between justice and compassion on the one hand (Engouang Ondo and Mor-Zamba), and expediency and cruelty on the other (Ntoutoume Mfoulou and Angone Zok, Jo The Juggler and Evariste), prevails in *Le*

Mvett and the Ruben cycle, particularly in *Lament*. Engouang Ondo must restrain his fellow warriors in the same way as Mor-Zamba must veto some of the most reckless initiatives of his two devoted companions.

Another similarity is the theme of the hero as a young orphan. Elone Kam Afe is an orphan who prevails despite the conspiracies of his malicious uncle, Bikuekue-bi-Loroto, against him. Mor-Zamba is the victim of a conspiracy by the same man who had already conspired to send his mother away from Ekoundoum. Engamba appears as a replica of Bikuekue-bi-Loroto, the image of a corrupt and selfish old man. Other similarities include stylistic features such as a fondness for long, overdrawn sentences with a predominance of verbs in the active form, controlled and expanded through a liberal use of adjectives. Both texts, while using action as the source of narrative energy, take on the exuberance of a bush fire. The dizzying pace of this action narrative is occasionally given cadence through the intervention of the *mbomo-mvet*, the performing artist meditating on his art. Whereas Ndoutoume laments the absence of a live *mvet* event and cries before the frustration of "playing the *mvet* on paper," Beti's narrator wonders about the nature of his art as he speaks directly to his audience and attempts to win their complicity.

Although it reiterates the fundamental teachings of the *mvet*, the Ruben cycle is not simply a repetition of the genre. The *mvet* is modified to espouse contemporary issues. Whereas justice and compassion are contrasted with expediency and cruelty through the tension of characters in *Le Mvett*, freedom and justice are contrasted with tyranny and oppression in the Ruben cycle. Whereas the narrative of *Le Mvett* adopts the fantastic mode as can be seen in the predominance of the metaphysical over the realistic, the Ruben cycle largely emphasizes the realistic mode, thereby giving preeminence to the historical over the fantastic. Although Akomo is present in both narratives, he is a dominant, acting figure in the *mvet* but distant and eventually forgotten in the Ruben cycle.

Finally, Beti may also be indebted to the *mvet* as a genre in orature, as a cyclical narrative with an enormous possibility for expansion. Contrary to such epics as *Sundiata*, *mvet* epics tend to be cyclical, bringing forth the same characters over and over again in a variety of new situations. While casting doubt on his ability to do so, Beti admitted that he would like to build a cyclical narrative, as did such nineteenth-century novelists as Balzac and Zola.[20] In reality, the tendency appears in his previous novels,[21] and with the Ruben novels, he has created a cyclical narrative that still offers a great potential for generative development. This effort originated from Beti's desire to deal more thoroughly with the depiction of the modern African scene. Beti believes that the fundamental function of the cyclical novel is to give its public a picture of its identity, a project that involves a vast description of a society at a given time and in such a way that its concerns are made clearly recognizable.[22]

Heroism in the Narratives

The heroic characters in the narratives under study symbolize a collective dream. Thus, when Ruben dies, Abena emerges as the new leader who continues the work left unfinished by the trade union leader; Abena gives impetus to the struggle, revitalizes it, and then disappears in the night. From then on, Mor-Zamba leads the liberation war. In the Mau Mau trilogy, Abdulla is the oldest and most experienced character among the major actors of Ilmorog. Munira, Wanja, and Karega cling to him and receive his teachings. By the end of *Petals of Blood*, they have played their parts in the conflicts of New Ilmorog, and the reader does not expect great actions from the trio of elders any longer. Munira is in jail; Abdulla is weakened by work and age; and Wanja seems to have retired, satisfied finally to be with child. The reader must turn to Karega, the college dropout who has become a unionist, for significant undertakings; but he is detained and accused of being a communist agitator. Nevertheless, the organized workers of Ilmorog recognize him as their leader and send a messenger to him in the detention camp.

The reader's attention also focuses on Joseph, the adopted son of Abdulla. He has grown into a young collegian involved in student activism. He is described holding in his hands "Sembene Ousmane's novel *God's Bits of Wood*, thus symbolically indicating the blueprint that will guide the younger generation of students and workers in the struggles of the future, in the same way in which Sembene Ousmane uses *La Condition Humaine* by Malraux in his novel.

The heroic character, it appears, must embody the aspirations of the oppressed. He must stand for those qualities that are seen as paramount by the best of his community. The heroic characters of Beti and Ngugi are dedicated to the realization of the quest for freedom and justice, and in pursuing this goal, they are made to emulate the best of their ancestral traditions.

In conclusion, it must be said that the writers stylize after the oral tradition in all possible ways, including the oral performance, however paradoxical the attempt may seem. How a novel could be stylized after an oral performance is difficult to imagine. In fact, it would be futile to try to match in writing the richness of an oral narrative. But the writers do not attempt this. Rather, they only seek to create an illusion of orature in their novels, as can be seen in *Lament*. The written narrative is presented as if it were an oral narrative transcribed by the author. It provides him with an additional means to create a distance between the text, as the collective narrative of the people of Ekoundoum, and the transcriber. This distance is meant to produce an illusion of authenticity in the text. Beti uses the word "audience" instead of "reader" as a pointer while allowing interventions from the narrator in the form of a discourse on the difficult nature of the task.

But whoever the narrator might be and as long as the story is being told separately by each participant, the *audience* will always have to tolerate a forgotten detail, an obscure point, and even, here and there, an unexplained break in the action or an incomprehensible turn of events. The *audience* itself is therefore obliged to redress these deficiencies either in the midst of the action or, more frequently, with displacement in time, because a new episode, a hitherto unclarified detail, or an anticipated allusion abruptly comes along to clear up a shadowy image that had been left behind long ago, just as a traveler who suddenly raises or lowers his torch often illuminates a thicket that had until then been shrouded in darkness.

What would happen if the various protagonists wanted to reach an agreement in order to offer the audience a coherent narrative of the events? Perhaps they would convey a better sense not only of its meaning, but also of its sequence and continuity; perhaps they would slow the momentum to a snail's pace, smooth out the steep slopes, and fence off the precipices. But before that occurs, they would have to battle it out so hard among themselves that they run an enormous risk of alienating each other permanently and never reappearing before the court. (*Lament*, p. 250; my emphasis)

This passage suggests that the writer is only a faithful recorder of the collective quest of the people of Ekoundoum as subsequently narrated by the actors of the quest themselves to members of their community. The concern for recording the quest of Ekoundoum is suggested toward the end of *Lament*, as the young schoolteachers begin to gather pieces of information on the "legendary" Abena, whose future return to his native city the Rubenists decide to stress; in doing so, they hope to keep the "legend" of Abena alive in the minds of the youth. Abena symbolizes the necessary heroic image that generates a sense of pride in the community; it serves to counterbalance the negative self-image that the regime of the despot chief had inculcated in the souls of the youth.[23]

Notes 5

[1] J. T. Shaw, "Literary Indebtedness," in *Comparative Literature: Method and Perspective*, ed. Newton P. Stallkencht Horst Frenz (Carbondale, Ill.: Southern Illinois University Press, 1973), 89.

[2] Eloise A. Brière, "*Remember Ruben*: Etude spatio-temporelle," *Présence Francophone*, no. 15 (1977): 32-33.

[3] Florence Stratton, "Narrative Method in the Novels of Ngugi," *African Literature Today*, no. 13 (1983): 123.

[4] Ibid.

[5] Ibid., 134.

[6] Aliko Songolo, "*Cahier d'un retour au pays natal* comme rite d'initiation," (Paper presented at the Congrès de L'AAFT [American Association of Teachers of French], Fort-De-France, Martinique, June 1979).

[7] J. P. Clark, *The Ozidi Saga*, (Ibadan: Ibadan University Press; Nigeria: Oxford University Press, 1977), xxviii.

[8] The neologism "orature" denotes poems, plays, and stories in oral form. For more information on the origin and usages of the word, see Chinwezu et al., *Toward the Decolonisation of African Literature* (Washington, D. C.: Howard University Press, 1983)

[9] Eno S. Belinga, *L'Epopée Camerounaise Mvet: Moneblum ou L'homme Bleu* (Yaoundé: Centre d'Edition et de Production Pour l'Enseignement et la Recherche, 1978). Tsira Ndong Ndoutoume, *Le Mvett I* and *Le Mvett II* (Paris: Présence Africaine, 1970-74).

[10] Rodger Mercier, M. Battestini, and S. Battestini, *Mongo Beti, ecrivain Camerounais. Textes commentes* (Paris: Fernand Nathan, 1964).

[11] Herbert Pepper, comp., *Un Mvet de Zwé Nguema, chant épique Fang*, republished by Paul and Paule De Wolf (Paris: Armand Colin, Classiques africains, 1972).

[12] So far, two models of presentation of orature in writing prevail. The model adopted by *Classiques africains*, described above, appears to be the "scholarly model" par excellence. The other model, which seems to be the favorite model of *Présence Africaine*, has offered books such as *Soundjata ou l'épopée mandingue*, *Le Mvett*, and *Le Maître de la parole*, epic stories from the repertoire of famous bards. These texts rarely bear the trademark of the "scholarly model." Although they may carry a short preface or introduction, they are not bilingual editions. Such texts can be said to belong to the "popular model," and in that sense, they share a common ground with books like *Contes d'Ahmadou Koumba* and *Le pagne noir*. Books published in the "popular model" are the result of oral material used in what Chinua Achebe calls "the way of the poet," which he aptly qualifies as the "dynamic way." See Chinua Achebe's "Achebe on Editing," *World Literature Written in English* 27 (1987):1-5.

[13] Ndoutoume, *Le Mvett*, 100-102.

[14] Ibid., 23.

[15] Ibid., 151-52.

[16] C. P. Ijomah and A. Kom, "Entretien avec Tsira Ndong Ndoutoume," *Présence Francophone*, no. 9 (1979-80): 174-82.

[17] Ibid., 177: "La femme dans le mvett constitue le secret dont on ne parle pas souvent."

[18] Ibid., 182: "la lutte véritable du mvett, c'est la lutte de soi-même, c'est-à-dire qu'il faut se retourner . . . Il (l'homme) lui faut trouver l'immortel qui est en lui-même . . . Il faut chercher à devenir immortel, par conséquent, lutter contre soi-même pour entrer dans soi."

[19] C. A. Kane, *L'Aventure ambiguë* (Paris: Julliard, 1961); Laye Camara, *Le regard du roi* (Paris: Plon, 1955); a N. Ngal, *Giambatista Viko ou le viol du discours africain* (Lubumbashi: Editions Alpha-Omega, 1975; reissued, Paris: Hatier, 1984); Kofi Awoonor, *This Earth, My Brother* (New York: Doubleday, 1971).

[20] Anthony Biakolo, "Entretien avec Mongo Beti," *Peuples Noirs/Peuples Africains*, no. 10 (July-August 1979): 86-121.

[21] Bernard Mouralis, *Comprendre L'oeuvre de Mongo Béti* (Paris: Editions Saint-Paul, 1981), 28.

[22] Biakolo, "Entretien," 119.

[23] In *The Wretched of the Earth*, Fanon indicates that the revival of such heroic figures serves to cement national unity during periods of crisis (New York: Grove Press, 1968).

6

Conclusion

Toward a New Cultural Awareness

The main objective of this study has been to interpret the Beti and Ngugi trilogies as a projection of a transformation myth. It has shown that central to any meaningful assessment of the works is a recognition of three related aspects of the authors' recent creative writing. The first is their use of popular myths and prophecies to lay a foundation for the whole narrative project. The myths trace the origins of the Essazam and of the Gikuyu peoples, and they outline a teleological vision. During social crises, the myths are subsequently reiterated by gifted visionaries in prophecies that predict the return and restitution of justice and freedom to the oppressed peoples. Sometimes the myths are unconsciously reenacted by leading characters or an entire community.

The second aspect is the writers' presentation of what I have called "the odyssey" of the communities in their quest for freedom. Here, the narrative brings into relief the historical dimension of the quest by carefully recording the social, economic, and mental transformations of the subjects. In addition to being narratives of heroic adventures, they incorporate the crucial use of what Tzvetan Todorov calls "le futur prophétique,"[1] a characteristic feature of the odyssey. The failure or successful realization of this prophetic future controls the narrative process. The odyssey in the Mau Mau and Ruben trilogies is also defined by the depiction of a long collective quest for freedom that culminates in armed insurrection and guerrilla warfare. Whereas Ngugi casts the trilogy in the unifying backdrop of the Mau Mau liberation war, Beti chooses to set his trilogy in the epoch of the U.P.C. guerrilla warfare led by Ruben Um Nyobe.

The trilogies also display a major innovation in the narrative style. Its dominant feature is the stylization of orature. The writers create the illusion of an oral narrative by presenting the stories to an imaginary listening audience instead of to readers. In addition, they use certain features of orature such as songs, praise names, and the archetypal structure of the traditional initiation process. Both writers adopt the narrative style of a master griot by using the authoritative voice of a collective narrator in an effort to create an epic atmosphere around their heroic narratives.

This style is counterbalanced by the novelists' use of the investigative method in *Perpetua* and *Petals of Blood* with murder cases to be solved. The method belongs primarily to the works that Todorov classifies among the suspense novels. Although past events are explored, the main focus of attention in the suspense novel is the exploration of the present situation of characters. This forms only the starting point of the story that must then answer the question of what is going to happen to the characters afterwards.

This choice shows that the narratives are not set in the exclusive epic mode. The presence of the investigative mode removes the formal and aesthetic crisis that the absolute certainty of the realization of the prophecies would cause and keeps the narratives in the realm of the novel and on the border of the epic.

Another similarity between the narratives is the evocation of creation myths and references to the gods of the Gikuyu (Ngai) and the Beti (Akomo). Equally important, however, are the use of prophets (Beti's the old man of Ekoundoum and Ngugi's Mugo wa Kibiro) and their prophecies in order to outline future developments in the trilogies; and the use of historical characters (Jomo Kenyatta and Ruben Um Nyobe) not only as leaders, but also as "shadow warriors" who are endowed with a messianic dimension in the narratives. The projection of a Pan-African vision in the narratives is supplemented by an attempt to bring into relief the identical aspects of Third World historical experiences such as colonialism and a heroic quest for freedom.

In Beti's trilogy, great figures of the African past are brought in the stories to add a significant scope to the novels' immediate world of reference, from the time of Akomo, the mythical founder of the nation, to his descendents and spiritual surrogates, such as Mor-Zamba, Abena, and Ruben. Outside of Cameroun, but still in Africa, political leaders of the African struggle for freedom, such as Kwameh Nkrumah, are mentioned. Finally, outside of Africa, reference is made to leaders of African descent who are an inspiration for the African quest for freedom in modern times. The impact of such historical figures as Toussaint L'Ouverture on the minds of Africans is registered in the heroic novel *Remember Ruben*. The Pan-African concern of the writer is quite explicit in the text.[2] Though not a new theme in African poetry, the attempt to link Africa and its diaspora can be seen as a new departure in its prose fiction.

In Ngugi's trilogy, the narrator brings in the narrative all the heroic figures of the Gikuyu past, such as Harry Thuku, Kenyatta, and Dedan Kimathi. In an effort similar to Beti's, Ngugi goes beyond Kenya to evoke a Pan-Africa symbolized by the road to be built across the continent to "Zaire, Nigeria, Ghana, Morocco, all over Africa" (*Petals*, p. 34). Abdulla, the old Mau Mau war veteran, becomes the griot who passes on to the youth the teachings of the heroic struggle of his generation (*Petals*, pp. 140-43). Beyond the African continent, numerous references are made to heroic figures of African descent in North America and the Caribbean, such as Nat Turner, Toussaint L'Ouverture, and Jean Jacques Dessalines. Heroic figures of Africa, such as Samori, Chaka, Eduardo Mondlane, Haile Selassie, Amilcar Cabral, and Gamal Abdal Nasser, join in a banquet of heroism.

Although heroic figures of the Pan-African world constitute the primary focus of the narrators in the novels of Beti and Ngugi, the reader also notes the presence of other anticolonial heroes from Asia and Latin America. In Beti's novels, the Third World is evoked at a greater distance through the tribulations of World War II veterans. Ngugi goes one step further and evokes the contributions of other Third World countries: the India of Mahatma Gandhi, the Chinese Revolution, the Latin America of "Che Guevara with his Christlike locks of hair and saintly eyes" (*Petals*, p. 161), and the Vietnamese liberation war.

A sense of identification with the societies whence the heroic figures of Latin America and Asia emerged is strongly suggested in the narratives. Indeed, we are quite far away from the all too familiar character whom the critics have labeled "le héros de l'aventure européenne." The only remnants of the theme of "European adventure" in these new narratives are the veteran World War II soldiers, like Joseph and Boro. But even these emerge in the narratives as underground supporters of independence. Indeed, Joseph and Boro are the builders of guerrilla armies. In a very important sense, Abena is the most glorified example of this new image of the war veteran.

The models used by Beti and Ngugi in their heroic narratives span the entire Third World; the aspirations appear to be identical. This is an extraordinary example of the writers' broad vision of the world. Nowhere else does one find such works of fiction today—novels that carry this worldwide vision of the unity of the oppressed. It is no small contribution to contemporary literature, given the gigantic stretch of vision demanded from artists whose work, although firmly rooted in their immediate lands, embraces continents well beyond their borders.

There are also differences between the two narratives. For example, Ngugi lays more emphasis on class conflict in his novels. This is central to *Petals of Blood*, where the narrative gradually focuses on the transformation of a small peasant environment into an industrial complex. One of the consequences of this transformation is the emergence of an industrial working class out of a mainly disinherited peasantry. Much of the narrative focuses on the opposition between the rich business class and the poor workers. This trend already appears in *Weep Not, Child* and *A Grain of Wheat*. Although Beti has had a continuous interest in the emergence of classes, the novels that form the Ruben trilogy do not emphasize class conflicts very much. In fact, *Lament* hardly makes any references to classes, apart from depicting the tense relations between a kind of colonial chieftain and a landless peasantry. This difference may reflect the present socioeconomic situations of each author's country, as Kenya has a larger industrial working class than Cameroun. A more likely explanation is that two of the Ruben novels (*Remember Ruben* and *Lament*) are set in the colonial era when little industrialization took place in Africa. But in *Perpetua*, Beti stresses the presence of a militaristic bureaucratic class, born to serve neocolonial interests.

Another difference appears in the depiction of women in the novels. Although they both describe the social conditions of women in male-controlled societies, Ngugi only seriously focuses on the theme in *A Grain of Wheat* and *Petals of Blood*. In contrast, Beti has kept a sustained interest in describing the social condition of women as victims of both colonialism and traditional African cultures as far back as 1956.[3] However, the female revolutionary militant appears much later in his writing. *Perpetua*, although a feminist novel in terms of central interest, is still the story of an essentially passive victim of a violent society. Moreover, Perpetua displays none of the strength and passion for freedom that Ngwane Eligui The Younger embodies in the liberation of Ekoundoum. At any rate, by the time the final novels of the trilogies were published, the two novelists developed a similar image of the revolutionary woman. Thus, they turned away from the widespread image of the woman as victim to depict the woman as revolutionary militant.[4]

Finally, the internal dynamic of the trilogies rests at all levels on the double itinerary of the subjects of the narratives. Failure and success are the two most dominant features of the trilogies. The Ruben trilogy registers the failure of the Rubenists to gain national independence despite their heroic struggle against the colonial forces. It also registers the country's drift into neocolonialism. This turn of events represents the negative phase in the quest of the subject of the narrative. The optimistic phase is underlined by the successful liberation of Ekoundoum by the Rubenists.

Ngugi displays the same pattern as Beti. *A Grain of Wheat* documents a successful struggle for political independence and the subsequent failure of the Mau Mau leadership to bring about profound transformations in the unjust relations of production established by settler colonialism. The novel records the birth of a local class that is a surrogate of the settler colonialists. While *Petals of Blood* describes the failure of Ilmorog peasants to protect their land, it also depicts the successful birth of a working class united by identical conditions.

Negative situations and positive realizations, an optimistic outlook after a pessimistic prospect, and failure and success appear during the quest of the subjects of the narrative trilogies. As works of fiction, the trilogies rest on creation myths. These creation myths serve as foundations on which the narratives unravel as transformation myths that mirror historical realities: the general modulation of the odyssey along popular uprisings and liberation wars, such as Mau Mau and U. P. C. guerrilla wars, and the particular aesthetic modulation of the transformational process itself. Creative imagination bridges the inevitable gap between sociohistorical realities and the visionary ideals of the writers. The profound desirability of salutary social changes that are within the realm of possible realization inspires the writers to create novels that offer themselves as positive social transformation myths. Yet the myths that the trilogies form are only agents that serve to give body and soul, to express vividly a vision of the transformational process toward the total—social, economic, and mental—emancipation of the subjects of the narratives. The ultimate transformation, necessarily, remains a historical process.

Notes 6

[1] Tzvetan Todorov, *Poétique de la prose, choix; suivi de Nouvelles Recherches sur le récit* (Paris: Editions du Seuil, 1978), 117.

[2] The Pan-African interest of Mongo Beti becomes even more obvious in a recent interview he gave in the daily newspaper *Le Soleil*. (See "Rencontre avec Mongo Beti: Pas de renaissance culturelle sans démocratie," interview by Anne-Jean Bart, *Le Soleil* [Dakar], 17-18 January 1987, p. 10. He revealed in this interview that he has been working on a dictionary of black cultures and black leaders worldwide. He announced that the book was to be published by L'Harmattan in Paris in October of 1987, but due to new discoveries he made regarding black cultures, leaders, and struggles in Latin America, it was decided to postpone the publication of the dictionary to a later date. The book has since been published: Mongo Beti and Odile Tobner, *Dictionnaire de la négritude* (Paris: Editions L'Harmattan, 1989).

[3] See Mongo Beti, *Le pauvre Christ de Bomba* (Paris: Robert Laffont, 1956), where the description of the *sixa* is an early sign of Beti's interest in depicting the social condition of women.

[4] Mohamadou Kane, "Le Féminisme Dans Le Roman Africain De Langue Française," *Annales de la Faculté des Lettres et Sciences Humaines*, no. 10 (1980): 199.

Bibliography

Primary Sources

Beti, Mongo [Eza Boto]. "Sans haine et sans amour." *Présence Africaine*, no. 14-15 (June-September 1953): 213-20. English translation, "Without Hate or Love." In *Jazz and Palm-Wine*, edited by Willfried F. Feuser, 175-84. Essex: Longman, 1981.

_____ [Eza Boto]. *Ville cruelle*. Paris: Présence Africaine, 1953. Portuguese translation, *A cidade cruel*. Lisboa: Edições 70, 1980.

_____. *Le pauvre Christ de Bomba*. Paris: Robert Laffont, 1956. English translation, *The Poor Christ of Bomba*. London: Heinemann, 1971. Portuguese translation, *O Pobre Cristo De Bomba*. Lisboa: Edições 70, 1980.

_____. *Mission Terminée*. Paris: Buchet/Chastel, 1957. English translation, *Mission to Kala*. London: Muller, 1958. Reprint. London: Heinemann, 1964.

_____. *Le roi miraculé*. *Chronique des Essazam*. Paris: Buchet/Chastel, 1958. English translation, *King Lazarus*. London: Muller, 1960. Reprint. London: Heinemann, 1970.

_____. *Perpétue et l'habitude du malheur*. Paris: Buchet/Chastel, 1974. English translation, *Perpetua and the Habit of Unhappiness*. London: Heinemann, 1978.

_____. *Remember Ruben*. Paris: Union Générale d'éditions, 1974. English translation, *Remember Ruben*. Ibadan: New Horn Press; London: Heinemann; Washington, D. C.: Three Continents Press, 1980.

————. *La ruine presque cocasse d'un polichinelle (Remember Ruben 2)*. Paris: Editions des Peuples noirs, 1979. English translation, *Lament for an African Pol*. Washington, D. C.: Three Continents Press, 1985.

————. *Les deux mères de Guillaume Ismael Dzewatama, futur camionneur*. Paris: Buchet/Chastel, 1983.

————. *La revanche de Guillaume Ismael Dzewatama*. Paris: Buchet/Chastel, 1984.

Ngugi wa Thiong'o [James Ngugi]. *Weep Not, Child*. New York: Macmillan, 1969.

————. *A Grain of Wheat*. London: Heinemann, 1971. French translation, *Et le blé jaillira*. Paris: Julliard, n.d. Portuguese translation, *Um grão de trigo*. Lisboa: Edições 70, 1980.

————. *The River Between*. London: Heinemann, 1974.

————. *Petals of Blood*. London: Heinemann, 1977. New York: E. P. Dutton, 1977. Portuguese translation, *Petales de Sangue*. Lisboa: Edições 70, 1980. French translation, *Pétales de sang*. Paris: Présence Africaine, 1985.

————. *Caitaani Mutharabi-ini*. Nairobi: Heinemann, 1980. English translation, *Devil on the Cross*. London: Heinemann, 1982.

————. *Matigari*. Nairobi: Heinemann, 1987. English translation, *Matigari*. London: Heinemann, 1989.

Ngugi wa Thiong'o and Ngugi wa Miiri. *Ngaahika Ndenda*. Nairobi: Heinemann, 1980. English translation, *I Will Marry When I Want*. London: Heinemann, 1982.

Secondary Sources

Awouna, Joseph. "Le conte africain et la société traditionnelle." *Présence Africaine*, no. 66 (1968): 137-44.

Barnett, Donald, and Karari Njama. *Mau Mau from Within*. New York: Monthly Review Press, 1966.

Baugh, Edward. "The West Indian Writer and His Quarrel with History." *Tapia* 7, no. 8 (1977): 6-7; *Tapia* 8, no. 9 (1977): 6-7, 11.

Belinga, Eno S. *L'Epopée Camerounaise Mvet: Moneblum ou L'homme Bleu*. Yaoundé: Centre d'Edition et de Production Pour l'Enseignement et la Recherche, 1978.

Bestman, Martin T. "Structure du récit et mécanique de l'action révolutionnaire dans *Remember Ruben*." *Présence Francophone*, no. 23 (1981): 61-77.

Beti, Mongo. "Lettre de Yaoundé: Cameroun 1958." *Preuves*, no. 94 (December 1958): 55-60.

_____. "Tumultueux Cameroun." *Preuves*, no. 103 (1959): 26-34.

_____. "Tumultueux Cameroun (II)." *Preuves*, no. 104 (1959): 30-39.

_____. *Main basse sur le Cameroun. Autopsie d'une décolonisation*. Paris: Maspero, 1972.

_____. "Identité et tradition." In *Négritude et tradition*, edited by Guy Michaud, 9-26. Bruxelle: Editions Complexes, 1978.

_____. "Le pauvre Christ de Bomba expliqué." *Peuples Noirs/Peuples Africains*, no. 19 (January-February 1981): 104-32.

Beti, Mongo, and Odile Tobner. *Dictionnaire de la négritude*. Paris: Editions L'Harmattan, 1989.

Biakolo, Anthony. "Entretien avec Mongo Beti." *Peuples Noirs/Peuples Africains*, no. 10 (July-August 1979): 86-121.

Biebuyck, Daniel, and Kahombo C. Mateene, eds. *The Mwindo Epic from the Bayanga (Congo Republic)*. Berkeley and Los Angeles: University of California Press, 1969.

Bird, Charles, with Mamadou Koita and Bourama Soumaoro. *The Songs of Seydou Camara, Volume One: Kambili*. Occasional paper in Mande Studies. Bloomington: African Studies Center, Indiana University, 1974.

Blair, Dorothy S. *African Literature in French.* Cambridge: Cambridge University Press, 1976.

Brière, Eloise A. "Remember Ruben: Etude spatio-temporelle." *Présence Francophone*, no. 15 (1977): 31-46.

―――. "La réception critique de l'oeuvre de Mongo Beti." *Oeuvres et Critiques*, nos. 3, 4 (1979): 75-88.

Chaffard, Georges. *Carnets Secrets de la décolonisation.* Vol. 2. Paris: Calmann-Levy, 1968.

Chinwezu, Owuchekwa Jemie, and Ihechukwu Madubuike. *Toward the Decolonization of African Literature.* Washington, D. C.: Howard University Press, 1983.

Clark, J. P. *The Ozidi Saga.* Ibadan: Ibadan University Press; London: Oxford University Press, 1977.

Durand, Gilbert. *Les Structures anthropologiques de l'imaginaire.* Paris: Bordas, 1969.

el Nouty, Hassan. "Anatomie de *Remember Ruben.*" Paper presented at the African Literature Association Annual Conference, Clairemont, Calif., 1981.

Eyinga, Abel. *Introduction à la politique Camerounaise.* Paris: Editions Anthropos, 1978.

―――. *Mandat d'arrêt pour cause d'élections.* Paris: L'Harmattan, 1978.

Innes, Gordon. *Sunjata: Three Mandinka Versions.* London: School of Oriental and African Studies, 1974.

Jabbi, Bu-Buakkei. "Conrad's Influence on Betrayal in *A Grain of Wheat.*" *Research in African Literatures* 2, no. 1 (1980): 50-83.

Joseph, Richard A. "Ruben Um Nyobe and the 'Kamerun' Rebellion." *African Affairs* 73, no. 293 (1974): 428-48.

―――. *Radical Nationalism in Cameroun.* London: Clarendon Press, 1977.

Kane, Mohamadou. "Le féminisme dans le roman africain de langue française." In *Annales de la Faculté des Lettres et Sciences Humaines*, no. 10 (1980): 141-200.

Kenyatta, Jomo. *Facing Mount Kenya.* London: Martin Seeker & Warburg, Ltd., 1938. Reprint. New York: Random House, 1961.

Killam, G. D. *An Introduction to the Writings of Ngugi.* London: Heinemann, 1980.

King, Bruce, and Kolowale Ogungbesan, eds. *A Celebration of Black and African Writing.* London: Oxford University Press, 1975.

Koinange, Mbiyu. *The People of Kenya Speak for Themselves.* Detroit: Kenya Publication Fund, 1955.

Kom, David. *Le Cameroun.* Paris: Editions Sociales, 1971.

Lindfors, Bernth. "Ngugi wa Thiong'o's Early Journalism." Paper presented at the African Studies Association Annual Conference, Los Angeles, Calif., 1978.

_____. *"Petals of Blood* as a Popular Novel." Paper presented at the African Literature Association Annual Conference, Clairemont, Calif., April 1981.

Masilela, Ntongela. "Ngugi wa Thiong'o's *Petals of Blood." Ufahamu* 9, no. 2 (1979): 9-28.

Mbembe, J. A., ed. *Ruben Um Nyobe, Le problème national Kamerunais.* Paris: L'Harmattan, 1984.

Meillassoux, Claude. "Le mâle en gésine ou De l'historicité des mythes." *Cahiers d'Etudes Africaines,* nos. 73–76 (1979): 353-80.

Melone, Thomas. *Mongo Beti: l'homme et le destin.* Paris: Présence Africaine, 1971.

Mercier, Roger, M. Battestini, and S. Battestini. *Mongo Beti, écrivain Camerounais. Textes commentés.* Paris: Fernand Nathan, 1964.

Monkman, Leslie. "Kenya and the New Jerusalem in *A Grain of Wheat." African Literature Today,* no. 7 (1975): 111-16.

Moore, Gerald. *Twelve African Writers.* Bloomington: Indiana University Press, 1980.

Mouralis, Bernard. "Aspects de l'écriture dans *Perpétue et l'habitude du malheur* de Mongo Béti." *Présence Francophone,* no. 17 (1978): 45-68.

_____. *Comprendre L'oeuvre de Mongo Béti.* Paris: Editions Saint Paul, 1981.

Nazareth, Peter. *Literature and Society in Modern Africa.* Nairobi: East African Literature Bureau, 1972.

Ndoutoume, Tsira Ndong. *Le Mvett I, II.* Paris: Présence Africaine, 1970-74.

Ngugi wa Thiong'o. *Homecoming.* London: Lawrence Hill & Co., 1972.

_____ [James Ngugi]. "The Return." Special Section on *Lotus* Laureates for the Year 1973. *Lotus: Journal of Afro-Asian Writing*, no. 19 (1974): 173-83.

_____. *Detained: A Writer's Prison Diary.* London: Heinemann, 1981.

_____. *Writers in Politics.* London: Heinemann, 1981.

_____. *Barrel of a Pen: Resistance to Repression in Neo-colonial Kenya.* Trenton, N. J.: Africa World Press, 1983.

_____. *Decolonizing the Mind.* London: Heinemann, 1986.

"Ngugi wa Thiong'o: Writer in Trouble," "Kamirithu: Future Looks Dim," "The Play That Got Banned." *The Weekly Review*, 9 January 1978.

Niane, Djibril Tamsir. *Sundiata: An Epic of Old Mali.* London: Longman, 1965.

Nkosi, Lewis. *Tasks and Masks: Themes and Styles of African Literature.* London: Longman, 1981.

Nkrumah, Kwameh. *Neo-colonialism, the Last Stage of Imperialism.* London: Heinemann, 1965.

Okpewho, Isidore. *The Epic in Africa.* New York: Columbia University Press, 1979.

Olney, James. *Tell Me Africa: An Approach to African Literature.* Princeton, N. J.: Princeton University Press, 1974.

Padmore, George. *Pan-africanism or Communism.* London: Denis Dobson, 1956.

Palmer, Eustace. *The Growth of African Literature.* London: Heinemann, 1980

Pepper, Herbert, comp. *Un Mvet de Zwé Nguema, chant épique Fang.* Republished by Paul and Paul De Wolf. Paris: Armand Colin, Classiques africans, 1972.

"Pour une mutation globale." Interview with René Depestre. *Poésie 1,* nos. 43-45 (January-June 1976): 79-88.

Robson, C. B. *Ngugi Wa Thiong'o.* London: Macmillan, 1979.

Rodney, Walter. "Problems of Third World Development." *Ufahamu* 3, no. 2 (Fall 1972). Reprinted in 11, no. 1 (Summer 1981): 115-32.

Sharma, Govind Narain. "Ngugi's Christian Vision: Theme and Pattern in *A Grain of Wheat.*" *African Literature Today*, no. 10 (1979): 167-76.

Songolo, Aliko. "*Cahier d'un retour au pays natal* comme rite d'initiation." Paper presented at the Congrès de L'AATF [American Association of Teachers of French], Fort-De-France, Martinique, June 1979.

Stallknecht, Newton P., and Horst Frenz, eds. *Comparative Literature: Method and Perspective.* Carbondale, Ill.: Southern Illinois University Press, 1979.

Storzer, Gerald. "Abstraction and Orphanhood in the Novels of Mongo Beti." *Présence Francophone*, no. 15 (1977): 93-112.

Stratton, Florence. "Narrative Method in the Novels of Ngugi." *African Literature Today*, no. 13 (1983): 122-35.

Todorov, Tzvetan. *Poétique de la prose, choix; suivi de Nouvelles Recherches sur le récit.* Paris: Editions du Seuil, 1978.

Voltaire. *Candide.* In *Romans et contes.* Paris: Garnier-Flammarion, 1966.

Wanjala, Christ. *For Home and Freedom.* Nairobi: Kenya Literature Bureau, 1980.

Wright, Edgar, ed. *The Critical Evaluation of African Literature.* London: Heinemann, 1973.

Kandioura Dramé, associate professor of French at the University of Virginia, studied at Université de Dakar and received his Ph.D. in comparative literature from the University of California at Los Angeles. His recent publications include "French Criticism of African Literature: On the Present State," in *African Literary Studies: The Present State/L'Etat Présent*, edited by S. Arnold, and "Social Function of Myth and Epic," in *Ufahamu*. He is associate editor for CARAF Books at the University of Virginia Press. Currently researching early African novelists, Dramé has also been involved in the translation and annotation of *Barlaban*, an important Mandinka epic poem.

This volume was edited and
composed on an Apple Macintosh
SE/30 using Microsoft Word 4.0
and PageMaker 3.02.
The final pages were produced
on an Apple LaserWriter Plus
and a Linotronic 100.

71572

DATE DUE

DEC 0 1 1994			
NOV 2 9 1994			
DEC 1 0 1999			
NOV 2 7 1999			
OCT 3 0 2001			
NOV 0 8 2001			
261-2500		Printed in USA